Foreword

For those of us with a more conventional metabolism, the pace and range of David Pickford's activity is almost frightening.

Like Johnny Cash, he's been everywhere, like Tintin, he's seen everything, like Thoreau, he's reflected hard on what a life on the wilder side might mean.

But David is not just a brilliant rock climber, capable alpinist, and committed adventurer who travels constantly. Despite a life lived in perpetual motion he edits magazines, writes articles and most of all takes photographs. I feel exhausted just thinking about it.

All these activities are included in this wide-ranging book, which ably illustrates not just his energy and creativity but his curiosity too. His intellect is no less restless than his body. Simply put, he wants to know why the universe is the way it is.

There's a tendency among those who knew climbing and travel before both activities became intensely commercialised to think that few of the current generation are engaged with the world around them, being more intent on raising their profiles than exploring their own inner lives.

I can't think of anyone who disproves this more thoroughly than David. It's like he's channelling Eric Shipton and Jack Kerouac while being thoroughly immersed in the concerns and energy of the present.

If there's any one section that stands out in this beautiful and often thought-provoking scrapbook from a twenty-first century nomad's saddlebag, then it is David's account of his motorcycle journeys across southeast Asia and around India. This is where my amazement becomes naked envy.

– Ed Douglas

I shall promote our going and coming, as shadows, in expressive light

– Geoffrey Hill

Introduction

A photograph is a passport to elsewhere, a place you may never have been before or where you may never go again.

The magic of photography transports us to these strange and familiar places, where it shows us what someone else, perhaps ourselves, once experienced through the eye of their camera. If we look at photographs, we dare to venture into time, that great creator and destroyer of humans, and to rediscover what another person once encountered. As we do, lighted fragments of the past are transformed into the most perfect illusions of reality ever made. And as they suspend our disbelief about their origins, meanings and representations, they enable us to be elsewhere with someone else.

Shakespeare said that there are seven ages of man. There are also seven deadly sins, seven samurai, and seven sisters. Interesting things, it seems, come in sevens. The sisters are a particular case in point, including cliffs in East Sussex, a station on the London Underground, a common name for the constellation of the Pleiades, a village in Wales, and the English name for a set of Stalinist skyscrapers in Moscow. By way of coincidence, perhaps, the majority of the photographs in this book were taken over a period of seven years. They are arranged in three sections.

The first, Glances, is a collection of landscape photography, in which I have chosen photographs that capture the elemental character of the places where they were made. When I am taking photographs in wild places, I am often astonished by the things my camera sees which I do not. Whilst I remain uncertain about the concept of photography as a form of art, I believe that through photographs we can discover something that is available to most of us yet only practised by a few: the art of seeing. As the great French photographer Henri Cartier-Bresson said, 'taking photographs is a means of understanding that cannot be separated from other means of visual expression. It is a way of shouting, of freeing oneself, not of proving or asserting one's originality. It is a way of life.'

The second, Dances, is a collection of climbing and adventure travel photography, and includes some essays and stories based on the featured images. And it is a portrait of some of the extraordinary people with whom I have been lucky enough to share the best experiences of my life – on the rocks, in the mountains, and among the world's wild places.

The third collection, Survivors, documents places, people, and things I have encountered that have survived the process sometimes called 'modernisation'. We live in an age of *neomania*, an aggressive condition in which the quest for the new seeks to exterminate the value of the old. Because this process has recently become so dramatic and so widespread, these images are an acknowledgement of the importance of that which does not need to be removed, upgraded, or replaced.

The wild places that still remain in our world are among the richest terrains for all kinds of adventure and discovery. Whilst I treasure the time I can be among these places, I also live in a city – just like most other people in the developed world. Reaching a balance with this paradox could be the biggest challenge facing anyone today who strives to lead an adventurous life. The Canadian writer Barry Lopez has said that 'one of the great dreams of man is to find some place between the extremes of nature and civilization where it is possible to live without regret'. To achieve this compromise, I use my camera to better understand why it is I must go climbing, travelling, and exploring.

John Berger reminds us that 'seeing… establishes our place in the surrounding world.' Photography, the most powerful technology of seeing ever devised, allows me to reach that elusive but somehow essential point of balance Lopez talks about. By understanding my experience of the elemental world through photography, I discover new methods of exploring it, new dimensions within it, and new reasons to value everything that lives, flourishes, and changes there.

As I do, the light elsewhere comes to life again, rising and falling anew.

Glances

A photograph is always invisible.
It is not it that we see.

– Roland Barthes

Colorado River from Deadhorse Point, Utah, USA

April 2010

Pines in rising light, Hingku Valley, Nepal

October 2007

Tsaranoro Be from the summit of Karimbony, Tsaranoro Massif, southern Madagascar

April 2008

Giant groundsels at circa 4000 metres, Kilimanjaro, Tanzania

February 2010

Leaf and shell, Thar Desert, Rajasthan, India

December 2005

Thorn tree in clearing light, Mendip Hills, Somerset, England

February 2009

The turn of the tide, Trebarwith Strand, Cornwall, England

November 2007

Electric storm, near Fianarantsoa, southern Madagascar. I made this photograph from a moving vehicle with a thirty second exposure and a 16mm lens. The area of orange light on the right was created by the headlights of a passing truck, and the thin white line on the left of the image is a flash of fork lightning that occurred just before the shutter closed. No Photoshop effects or other digital manipulations have been deployed on the image. I took around 50 frames of this powerful, five-hour storm before making this single, successful shot.

April 2008

Meadow above the Tsarap river in an incoming thunderstorm, near Phuktal, Zanskar Range, northwest India

August 2006

A full moon rising above part of the long and complex south ridge of Chamlang (7319m), Khumbu, Nepal. Through this telephoto image, the vast bulk of Kanchenjunga (8,586m), the world's third highest mountain, and also the summit of Jannu (7710m) can be clearly seen in the far distance in the centre-right of the photograph, through the prominent col.

October 2007

Moonrise above a cloud inversion in the high Khumbu, Nepal. The striking summit left of centre is Chamlang (7319m) and in the distance on the very far left is Makalu (8481m), the world's fifth highest mountain. This photograph was taken approximately twenty minutes after the image on the facing page. The two images show the remarkable colour shift that takes place at high altitudes at sunrise and sunset.

October 2007

Evening light on the west face of Makalu (8,481m), the world's fifth highest mountain, Khumbu, Nepal. The direct line up the sunlit face to the left of the prominent spur in the centre (the West Pillar, climbed by a French team in 1971) remains unclimbed, and is one of the greatest unsolved high altitude challenges in world mountaineering.

October 2007

Sudden shadow on Hay Bluff, Herefordshire, England

March 2009

Waterfall and balanced stone, lower Hingku Valley, Nepal

October 2007

Ice circle, Lynn Idwal, Snowdonia, Wales

January 2010

Red and purple over green, Westonbirt, Gloucestershire, England

November 2012

Lenticular cloud near Imilchil, High Atlas, Morocco

January 2003

Turning maple at Glacier Point, Yosemite Valley, California, USA

October 2006

Blue pods of Decaisnea Fargesii, Westonbirt, Gloucestershire, England

November 2010

Poppy in a field of wheat, Norfolk, England

July 2008

Boulder on a volcanic plain, northeast Iceland

July 2007

Two islands (Favignana and Marettimo) rising at sundown, Sicily, Italy

April 2013

Two hills (Moel Cynghorion and Moel Eilio) in falling light, Snowdonia, Wales

April 2007

The sun, coming hard around the world:
the island rises from the sea, sinks, rises, holds

— Peter Matthiessen, *Far Tortuga*

Evening falling over Lynn Du'r Arddu, Snowdonia, Wales

April 2007

Last light over Canyonlands and the La Sal Mountains, Utah, USA

April 2010

Evening light leaving the summit of the Totem Pole, Monument Valley, Arizona, USA

April 2010

Late sun and cloud-smoke on Kilimanjaro's Uhuru Peak (5895m), the highest mountain in Africa, Tanzania

February 2010

Windbound hawthorn, Exmoor, England

September 2009

Summit cairn frosted with snow-ice, Waun Fach, Brecon Beacons, Wales

January 2013

Giant groundsel and descending mist at circa 4300 metres on the western slopes of Kilimanjaro, Tanzania.
This remarkable habitat of mature high altitude vegetation is one of the world's highest cloud forests.

February 2010

30

Last light on Castleton Tower, Castle Valley, Utah, USA. The obvious narrow corner in shadow on the sunlit face is the line of the *Kor-Ingalls Route* (5.9), featured in Allen Steck and Steve Roper's book *Fifty Classic Climbs of North America*. Castleton Tower is the most famous of hundreds of Windgate sandstone towers on the Colorado Plateau in southern Utah, one of North America's best areas for adventurous rock climbing.

April 2010

Dike on a summer evening, Cambridgeshire, England

July 2008

River on a winter morning, near Vallouise, Ecrins Massif, France

January 2008

Rainbow over the Andringitra National Park in an incoming thunderstorm, Tsaranoro Massif, southern Madagascar

April 2008

Parabolic cloud over Mont Blanc du Tacul in a descending storm, Mont Blanc Massif, France.
I was skiing the Petit Envers route down the Vallée Blanche with Jonathan Griffith and Will Sim when a warm front came in from the south and the weather changed from cloudless skies to high winds and very low visibility within an hour.
We skied out at a snail's pace between big crevasses and on disappearing tracks in the cloud-filled gloom. This photograph always reminds me of just how fast and how dramatically the weather can change in the high mountains.

January 2010

Turret Arch and the La Sal Mountains on a spring evening, Arches National Park, Utah, USA

April 2010

Vernal Fall from the Mist Trail, Yosemite National Park, California, USA

October 2006

Am Buachaille from Sandwood Bay in a rising sea, Northern Highlands, Scotland

August 2007

Clearing storm over the Peuterey Ridge, Mont Blanc, Italy

January 2007

Dying glacier at circa 5500 metres near the summit of Uhuru Peak, Kilimanjaro, Tanzania. Kilimanjaro's glaciers have retreated very dramatically in the last fifty years, with an 85% reduction in their size between 1912 and 2007.

February 2010

Sudden sunbeam, Cape Cornwall, England

September 2007

Clearing squall, Somerset Levels, England

February 2007

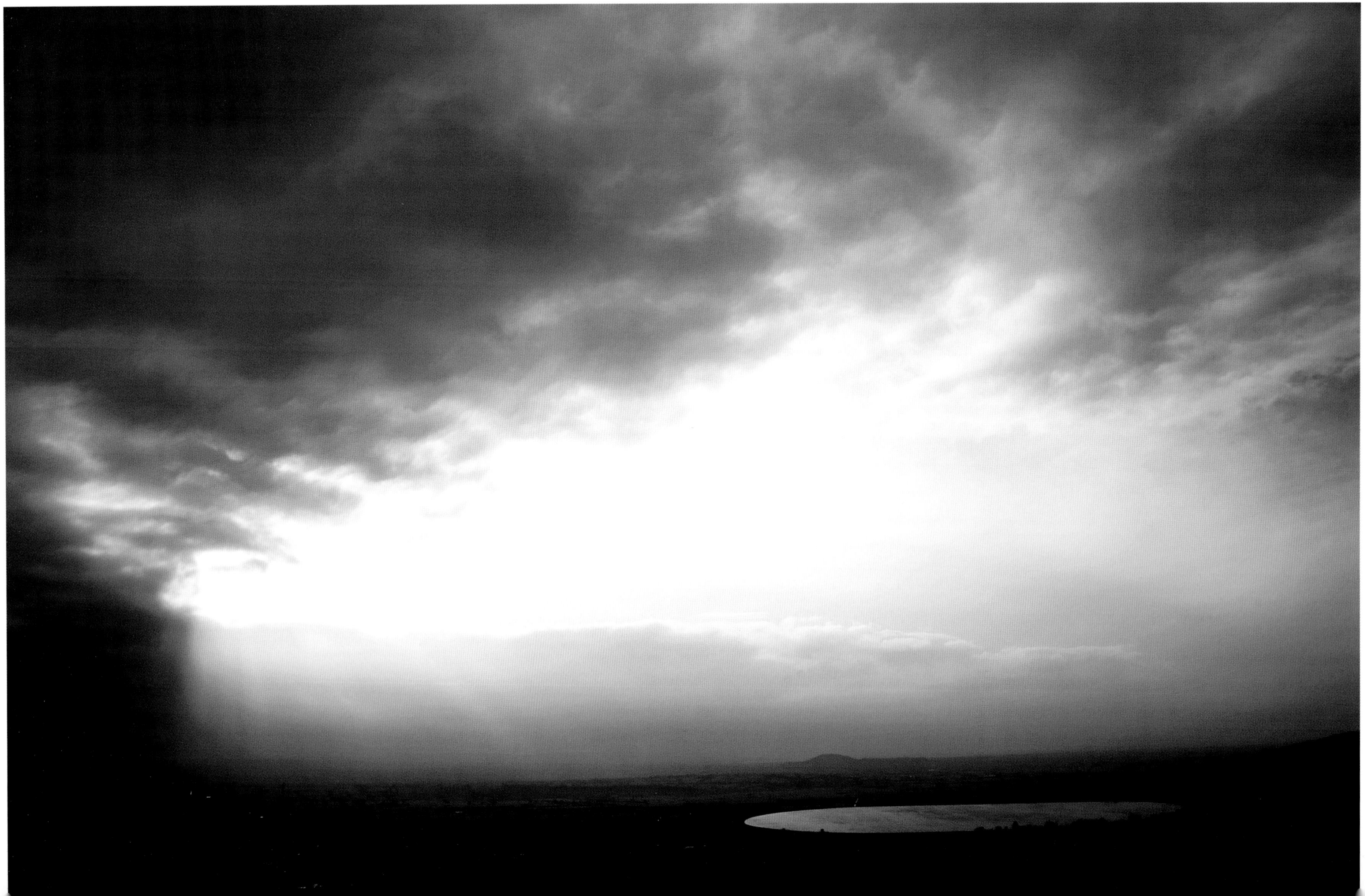

Summer storm over the Dent de Morcles, Petit Muveran and Grand Muveran, Valais, Switzerland

July 2012

Late sunlight on the West Face of Mera Peak (6476m), Hingku Valley, Nepal

October 2007

Summer sky, Callala Bay, New South Wales, Australia

December 2012

Sea-squall at dead low tide, Barafundle beach, Pembrokeshire, Wales
December 2012

Monument Valley, Arizona, USA

April 2010

Emergent thunderheads at dawn from circa 5000 metres over the Serengeti Plain, Tanzania.

The great French aviator, adventurer, writer and poet Antoine de Saint-Exupéry (author of *Wind, Sand, and Stars*) disappeared over the Mediterranean in July 1944 on his last reconnaissance mission.

This photograph reminds me of his extraordinary life, his mysterious death, and his books; particularly his second novel *Night Flight,* which he based on his experiences of flying mail planes over Argentina in the 1930s.

February 2010

Blue and red form, Punta di Capineru, Corsica, France

May 2006

White and blue form, Capo Testa, Sardinia, Italy

May 2005

Lenticular cloud at sunset, Todra Gorge, Atlas Mountains, Morocco

January 2003

Pampas grass on an autumn morning, Catalunya, Spain

November 2010

Breaking wave, Sennen, Cornwall, England.
A second after I made this photograph I was completely drenched by the wave, standing on the clifftop thirty metres above the sea. It captures the raw, colossal power of the ocean.

September 2007

Avalanche in motion, Upper Hingku Valley, Nepal.
To get a sense of scale, the boulders in the avalanche's path are the size of average semi-detached residential houses.

October 2007

Breaking surf by starlight, Ringstead Bay, Dorset, England

May 2009

Detail of Vernal Fall, Yosemite National Park, California, USA

October 2006

Boulder and sea ice, Hönö, Västra Götaland, Sweden: midwinter, northern Europe

February 2011

Three ridges, Andalucia, Spain:
midwinter, southern Europe

January 2012

Last light leaving the summit of Mont Blanc, Chamonix, France

January 2012

The south face of L'Aiguille du Midi after a three day winter storm, Chamonix, France

January 2012

Dancing flags above the ruined ramparts of Sankar Gompa, Ladakh, India

August 2009

Purple hill near Rumbak, Zanskar Range, India

August 2009

Lone shrub and shifting dunes, western Thar desert, Rajasthan, India

December 2005

Nigeen Lake, Srinagar, Kashmir, India

December 2005

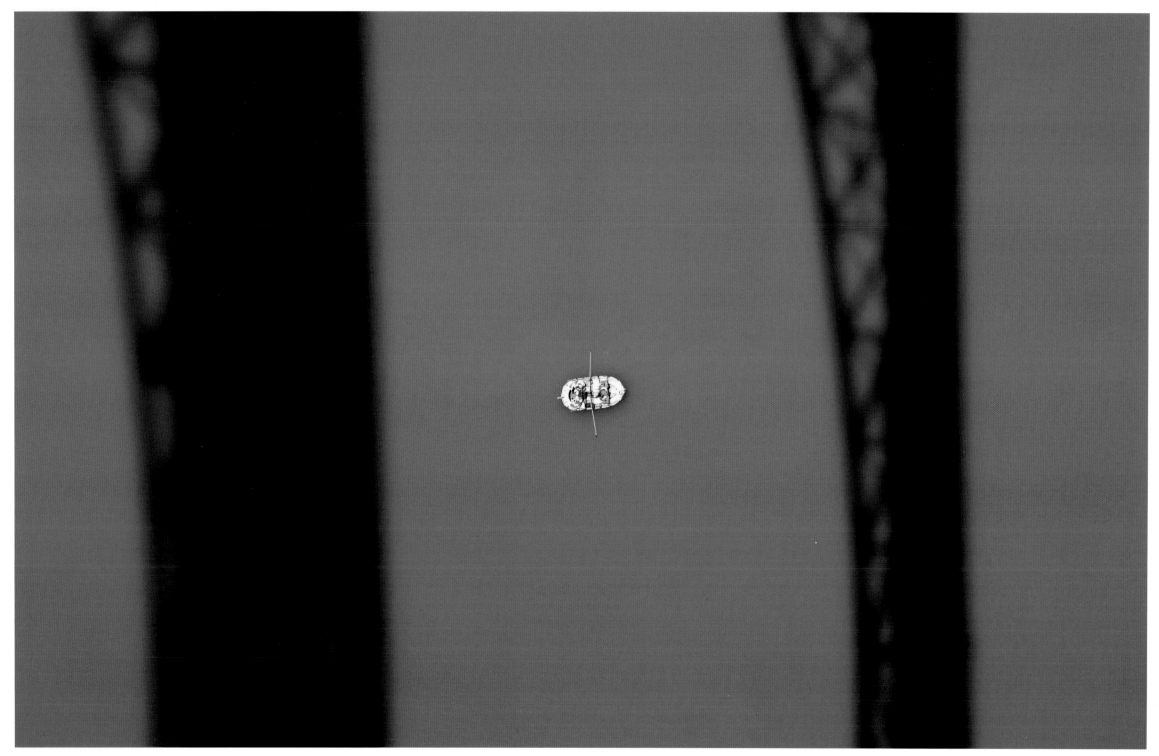

Heading downriver under the Navajo Bridge, Marble Canyon, Arizona, USA

April 2010

Summer's end, Bohuslän, Sweden

September 2010

Approaching storm over Helbronner, Mont Blanc, France

January 2010

Afternoon shadows on the summit crest of Cosmiques Couloir, Mont Blanc, France

January 2010

Last light on the Carneddau, Ogwen Valley, Snowdonia, Wales

January 2010

Glade of the living and the dead, Westonbirt, Gloucestershire, England
November 2010

A dusting of snow on solidified magma near the summit of Kilimanjaro's Uhuru Peak (5895m), the highest mountain in Africa, Tanzania

February 2010

Wild poppies at the edge of an open field, Norfolk, England

July 2008

Pink rain over the Colorado River, Canyonlands, Utah, USA

April 2010

Sudden light on Broad Bench and Kimmeridge Bay, Isle of Purbeck, Dorset, England

January 2009

Three skiers, Vallée Blanche, Mont Blanc, France

January 2012

Two ridges above the summer pastures of Nimaling, Zanskar Range, northwest India

August 2009

Dances

This dance has no name.
It is a hungry dance.

– Wallace Stevens

Tim Emmett pulls through the crux roof of *Dominatrix* (7c) Kilnsey Crag, Wharfedale, North Yorkshire, England

July 2008

Jack Geldard makes the second ascent of *Pre-Cambrian Wrestler* (E7 6b) at Penlas Rock, South Stack, Gogarth, Anglesey, Wales. When Jack and I repeated this awesome George Smith creation, we were astonished by just how steep and strenuous it was, overhanging about fifteen metres in total. George Smith is a renowned specialist at steep, physical, and geologically strange climbs requiring sophisticated solutions. This type of rock climbing has become unfashionable in recent years.

James Harrison nears the top of the second pitch of the classic cascade *Davidoff* (WI 5), Fournel Valley, Ecrins Massif, France.
The Fournel Valley is one of the best places in Europe for ice climbing, with hundreds of frozen waterfalls of all grades, aspects, and lengths.

January 2008

A climber reaches the crux section of *El Delphin* (7c+), Las Ventanas del Mascún, Rodellar, Spain. Rodellar's Mascun gorge, which runs south from the Sierra de Guara mountains in northern Aragon, is one of the most popular places in Europe for high standard limestone sport climbing. This remarkable climb follows the inner spur of the arch known as 'The Dolphin', for obvious reasons.

October 2008

Giles Cornah gains the icicle of *Sombre Heroes* (WI5) after an ascent of *Prends Moi Sec* (M7+) at Ceillac in the Ecrins Massif, France. The route gains the icicle after a wild trip through the large cave to its left. It is typical of the modern style of athletic 'mixed' climbs which involve the use of ice axes and crampons to ascend steep rock with hanging ice structures.

February 2008

'The edge of land: a place where the light changes, where people change.' Steve Monks in the open groove of the classic Cornish extreme *Raven Wall* (E3 5c) at Bosigran, Cornwall, England

May 2007

Sea Change

Notes from the Edge of Land

Desire is a strange hotel, a place of echoes and half-opened doors. On a late monsoon morning in Pulau Nias, Indonesia, from an outrigger canoe, I watched the vapour lift and stir over the rainforest. Half visible within it, a dark sheet of volcanic rock rose from the palms and tangled creepers, steepening with height. At once, the memory of an unclimbed headwall on Cornwall's north coast flashed back at me, like quartz by moonlight. I began to conjure up the line: a spidery crack; an incipient flake, fading out; a traverse left, perhaps, along a smooth shelf.

When I was fourteen years old, I'd run down that steep seaward slope, my gaze fixed as the Great Wall of Pentire Head reared from the waves. My friend Paul must have noticed how the wall had entranced me, because he handed me the lead on both pitches of *Eroica* (E3), the classic line up the huge flake that splits the heart of the crag. At the top of the final lieback groove, I paused in balance. Under my hands, the frozen magma, traced with delicate veins, fused and made visible the ancient life of the earth. It was as if a fault had cracked open.

Once you've cast adrift on a sea cliff, there's no quick retreat. That day's enchantment had directed my life as a climber, taking me from Cornwall on to Europe, then Africa, Central Asia and eventually the East. Now, ten years later, as I peered through the mist at the sheet of dark stone emerging from the jungle, the longing to return home resounded hard.

The edge of land: a place where the light changes, where people change. I went to high school in Oxford, about as far inland as you can get in England. The cloistered towers and narrow streets oppressed me, as did the expectations of playing football and dating. Friday afternoons, I'd escape the city with a driven urgency, headed for the coasts of western England and Wales—where, between the mirrored vastness of sky and water, I became part of a visible world that extended beyond reckoning.

One June morning after my last exams, I jumped on a train to meet Mike Robertson for a week's climbing on Lundy Island. From Ilfracombe, a small harbour town on Devon's north coast, the Oldenburg sails for a tiny granite island twelve miles offshore, and the home of some of the best sea cliff climbing in Europe.

I woke to the sound of gulls, and waited on the quay as wooden boxes were loaded in the hold. The west wind blew straight off the Atlantic, full of brine and salt. Quickly, the ocean took hold of my senses, replacing the reams of algebra and lines of Shakespeare that had occupied my past weeks: 'Full fathom five thy father lies / And of his bones are coral made; / Those are pearls that were his eyes; / Nothing of him that doth fade, / But doth suffer a sea-change / Into something rich and strange.'

The Oldenburg cast out beyond the harbour and into the tidal stream. The men working on the boat had deeply wrinkled faces, drawn by years of running the tides around southwest England. I felt a premonition of my own sea change from schoolkid to climber. By the time we dropped anchor in the bay on the island's southern tip, the tide had begun to turn again, ebbing now.

Mike had left a note in the campground: 'See you at Landing Craft Bay, we'll be there until late.' Too excited to walk, I ran across the fields past the Old Light and scrambled down the undercliff to where Mike and the others had stashed their gear. As I clipped in to the seventy metre static line to rappel down to the boulders, the exam room that had encased me earlier in the week faded altogether.

A line of low clouds built up in the west. Mike moved rapidly across the strongest line through the centre of the granite slab: *Matt Black* (E4). He stopped at a faint weakness and coaxed in a tiny microwire. I was so engrossed in watching his progress that when the first wave splashed my rock shoes I thought it had started to rain. A second later, I registered its source: the tide! After Canada's Hudson Bay, the English and Welsh coasts of the Bristol Channel have the largest tidal range on earth. This, coupled with the Channel's funneling effect, has caught out countless climbers unaware.

As Mike pulled through the final moves, his last gear fifteen metres below him, I scurried from the water's reach, aiming for a tiny ledge at seven metres. By now, the ropes were a swirling, blue-green mass in the cove, like the tentacles of a gigantic octopus. I rocked up on the tiny ledge just as a bigger wave came in, completely submerging the boulders where I'd been anchored a few moments earlier. With just enough room to swap feet, I wrung the seawater from each of my shoes, balancing precariously on the ledge with the other. Within minutes I was leaving a trail of wet prints on the smooth rock.

David Pickford (leading) and David Moore on the first ascent of the bold slab climb *Daddy Cool* (E8 6b) at Carreg y Barcud, North Pembrokeshire, Wales

May 2005 (photo | Sarah Garnett)

A bank of cloud rolled in over the ocean, thickening the fading light. I was like a child who'd run toward the sea's jaws, enthralled by the peril of the breaking wave, then raced back, filled with fear and delight. In that instant before I'd fled, I'd felt myself edging along a polished shelf separating existence and desire, aware of another world that lay beyond them both.

At nineteen, with more energy for climbing than I could usually expend in one day, I was often overtaken by the ocean or by darkness. Late one August evening at Bosigran, Mark Glaister declared he was ready for a cup of tea. Mark, who had introduced me to Cornish granite, was older and far more sensible than I. After we'd packed up our gear I ran back, alone, all the way from the Carn Galver mines to the top of the Great Zawn and slid down a static line to the base of *Desolation Row* (E2).

The heat of the day had given in to lengthening shadows. I began climbing almost immediately, enthralled by the freedom of moving quickly without ropes or gear. Soon I was high on the slab, balancing on small edges below the crux section, where the crack thins into a spidery seam. The sea glinted darkly from the cavern below, slurping between the boulders. Somewhere overhead, a peregrine shrieked. Lifted by its call, the offshore wind blew huge eddies beyond Bosigran Head and north toward Carn Gloose. I raced back over to the Main Cliff and up Joe Brown's 1957 masterpiece, *Bow Wall* (E2). As I swung from the perfect handjam at the end of the diagonal crack, a rush of feathers whistled past my shoulder and fell through the 200 feet of space below. The peregrine had returned.

I scampered back down *Doorpost* (HS) in the gloom. Soon, I was chalking up below the thin crack of *Suicide Wall* (E1) in the heart of the cliff. It was almost nightfall when I reached the top for the final time.

Huge, parabolic boulders rest on the summit of Bosigran Head like slumbering sea-monsters. Dawn and dusk seem to animate them back to life. I stretched out flat on one of them, feeling the immensity of time in the sharp crystals under my fingers. The air was still. Far out to sea the offshore wind carved whorls in the darkening water. My eyes adjusted, and the sky crackled with stars.

Three summers later, high on *Bosigran Ridge* (VD) – a great jagged line of upturned fangs rising from Porthmonia Cove for 300 metres – I looked back as my partner, Sarah, appeared and vanished, emerging again as a faint, dark shape on the crest.

As I watched her shadow moving against the swirling air, my own was superimposed against the cloud, weird and unreal. It was a rare sea cliff version of a brocken spectre, the natural doppelganger that haunted early alpinists. Edward Whymper, descending the Matterhorn after the deaths of his four companions, had been spooked by those preternatural silhouettes.

In German folklore, to meet your 'double walker' is a portend of destruction. The English Romantic poet Shelley saw his, adrift in a storm off Italy in the Don Juan, and never returned alive. I shuddered, thinking of how mountains are just like the sea, most beautiful when most deadly. Hermann Buhl, high on Chogolisa; the serac falling like a breaking wave. Alison Hargreaves near the summit of K2; the storm encasing the high Karakoram like ocean fog. Brendan Murphy, descending Changabang; that spindrift avalanche catching him like a gust of windblown sand. In the places of our greatest inspiration, death is often a quick companion, a shadow-watcher flashing through the vivid dark.

Later that year, November came on fast through the autumn rain. London evaporated. On the plane over Siberia, the crystal grid of Novosibirsk sparked back at me through the winter night, and I closed my eyes. Hong Kong opened and shut like a clam in the tidal current. Women were hanging out their sheets on the balconies of apartment blocks, like white sails swirling in the sun. When I boarded my plane to Hanoi, a red flag with a five-pointed star in its centre shimmered through the static on the departures screen. Philip Larkin's poem came into my mind about the ship that 'went wide and far/ Into an unforgiving sea/ Under a fire-spilling star./ And it was rigged for a long journey.'

Four months later, the hills and deltas of East Asia I'd travelled through on my Vietnamese-registered Minsk faded into a dream-sequence, locked up with the battered motorcycle in the chandler's shed by the pier at Ko Laoliang, a tiny island in the Surin Archipelago about twenty miles off Thailand's southwest coast. Here, I'd met up with ex-pat American Mike Weitzman and Trev Massiah, a climbing friend from home. We'd found a hundred-metre wall of unclimbed limestone, honeycombed with caves and draped with gigantic tufas, rising straight from a beach of tide-washed sand – a perfect climber's playground. It was exactly the break I needed from the road, but when my friends had to leave, I headed south for Indonesia, the idea of a climax to my journey, and the sea.

On a red evening full of dusty rain in southern Sumatra, I followed the road to Danu Ranau, where an ink-dark lake broods beneath a tall volcano. There, narrow rice fields cling to the water's edge. That was what I wanted: to draw a life from both land and water, existence and desire. At that point in my journey, a current swept through me, stronger than any I'd yet encountered: it was too strong even to stop and climb. Each day, I'd be on the bike by dawn, and travel by instinct. Most days, I'd ride on into the dark after the evening mist had swirled low over the rice fields. I rode north, to Aceh, east to the high country of Java, and back to Sumatra and the Indian Ocean.

A few weeks later, I waited on the quay at Sibolga for the night boat to Pulau Nias. In Sorake Bay I stayed in a small wooden shack on stilts by the low stone breakwater under the first line of coconut trees.

It belonged to Raul, who'd built it before his first son was born sixteen years ago. The first morning, I woke to an oily sun recoiling off the triple-overhead surf that broke hard on the outer reef, and the chatter of Raul's youngest son trying to help his sister fix her bicycle in the yard. By evening, the surf was as loud as a low-flying plane. The village kids from Sorake raced around with enormous sticks, whistling and laughing, trying to capture fugitive coconuts.

The next day in Sorake, I met Mr Gurung, a local fisherman.

As his outrigger canoe broke through the first band of surf, he removed his tattered shirt to wring the water from it. Long ropes of muscle stretched across his thin frame. I blinked: a scar started behind his left shoulderblade and ran unbroken down the front of his chest, across his torso and halfway down his right thigh.

'What is it?' I asked.

'A big shark' he replied. A wide, boyish smile spread across his face, deepening the strong wrinkles from sixty-two years spent mostly between the ocean and the sky.

How the hell did he survive that? The shark's bite radius couldn't have been less than a metre twenty. The smile on Mr Gurung's face had widened further, lighting up his dark eyes with a sudden, wild laughter that said 'Yes, I know.'

I'd thought I knew about the sea and its wildness. But his life— and the lives of most coastal Indonesians—had been more profoundly marked and shaped by the sea than anything I'd encountered. For me, the coast was the place I'd found inspiration as a climber. Mr Gurung and his fellow fishermen ventured into more hazardous waters, in search of the oldest source of life itself.

In the outrigger a few days later, Mr Gurung caught a big kingfish on the trailing tackle. That twisting blade of colour lifted my eyes from the sea, and I looked inland. Vapour wreathed the tallest trees. Then that dark sheet of volcanic rock appeared, reminding me of that unclimbed line on the headwall of Pentire's Great Wall in Cornwall.

Mr Gurung paddled back toward the beach. The hull of the canoe growled into a sand bar. I looked up again, and the wall had vanished. That was what I wanted to figure out: how to draw life from both land and water, existence and desire. If I could return to my original point of departure with new eyes, I thought, perhaps I could finally unlock its mystery. But such finality confounded me with strangeness: the unforgiving future of adventuring, of setting out.

Three weeks later, in a small town in Malaysia's central highlands, I logged on to my email for the first time in over a month. A message from Mike Robertson flashed up in bold at the top of the page, untitled. It was unlike him not to title a mail. Cold fear swirled through me.

'Damian Cook's drowned off Devil's Cove' the email read. 'His funeral will be in two weeks. Sorry to have to write to you about this. Take care out there. Mikey.'

Trevor Massiah crossing the crux roof of his own route *Fool's Gold* (7b), Ko Laoliang, Surin Archipelago, southwest Thailand. Trevor and I, along with American Mike Weitzman, spent several weeks opening new routes on this 100 metre wall of honeycombed orange limestone rising from the island's only beach in spring 2004. There are now more than fifty climbs on the island's east coast.

March 2004

'To be a voyager between worlds': Bob Hickish shadow-dancing into the light on the second ascent of Pete Oxley's masterpiece *Palace of the Brine* (8a+) in the gigantic, secret sea-cave at Fisherman's Ledge, Swanage, Dorset, England

July 2009

Our friend had been caught in a powerful cross-current after pitching off a deep water solo in Mallorca. He was a strong swimmer, but the sea was stronger that day. I paid my bill in silence and walked out. The evening smelled of dust and rain. My voyage out was over.

After Damian's funeral, I returned to Pentire alone. A passionate exponent of bold climbing, Damian would have loved the idea of my route: a faint, inescapable line of weakness through the most imposing piece of rock on the crag. He'd have wanted it to rise straight from the ocean, too.

The morning's squalls had cleared and the blade-sharp air washed the city from my senses. I threw a hundred-metre static line out across the overhanging upper wall. A gust of wind trapped it in mid-arc. For a moment the rope was held in equilibrium, quivering slightly. Three hundred feet below, a massive swell threw spray halfway up the cliff.

I rappelled down to the lip of the headwall. The wind twirled me around like a string puppet before I could catch an edge and place a tiny wire to hold the rope close to the rock. I peered down at the smooth sheet of stone below, gently overhanging for twenty metres. Tight, tiny swirls of quartz distracted my attention from the almost complete lack of gear placements. Sawn-off knifeblades bounced from the minute cracks into which I tried to coax them. One protruded from a horizontal seam by almost a centimetre, and I tied it off.

Far out to sea, shadows of clouds crossed the water. I remembered how Damian had laughed when I'd said a particular crux above deep water was too high, that anything above sixty feet was just like soloing above ground. 'It's not about the height, Dave. It's about relaxing. Just relax. Just be free up there.'

He would have loved this spot. Maybe this was how you got past desire's half-opened door: by finding those places and instances where life and death collide so intensely that they break apart, letting you slip through, momentarily, unnoticed. Like a magician. Or a ghost.

Ten metres above the terrace, as I poked the nose of a carabiner into a shallow depression, it disintegrated to reveal an open pocket. A 2.5 cam just sank into it, the teeth biting against the gritty quartz. The wall afforded this one concession. Then, before I could even chalk up, the first heavy splats of a summer squall hit the rock. Rain sheeted across southwest England through August, and it was several weeks before I could return.

On a cool September morning, I rapped down for the third time. Mike Robertson was already anchored in the niche, uncoiling the ropes, just as attentive as on our first day climbing together. A fulmar squawked, firing a neat globule of regurgitated fish at him. He ducked from the shoulder and laughed it off. His quiet self-confidence and strength pervaded the air along the narrow terrace.

'Where's the cam, Mikey?' I asked, in a moment of pre big-lead amnesia.

'On that sling you've just clipped to red, you young rascal!'

Suddenly I was moving, as a gust of wind curled across the crag. My fingers hit a crimp. Before I could fully register what I was doing, I irreversibly left the sanctuary of the pocket, casting adrift on the headwall, moving quickly between small edges. My ropes trailed out, jarring brightly against the dark rock. Far below, the hiss and gurgle of the sea disappeared. Even the cawing gulls fell quiet, and I entered a space of vivid silence with no beginning or end in time.

Then, without warning, I was in balance once more, this time crouched on the arête that defines the headwall's limit. Tiny quartz edges bit into my skin as I glanced back down at Mike. Below, the ocean streamed with strands of gigantic seaweed. Mike's quiet voice folded into the crash of the next wave, and the world I'd left behind returned, suddenly made new.

They say the wave looked small at first, just a strange, wide line beyond the broad circumference of the reef. When it hit the west coast of Nias, it was metres high. The Boxing Day tsunami on December 26th, 2004, killed 140 Niasans and about 225,000 people on the coasts of Sumatra, Thailand, Sri Lanka and India—the world's deadliest recorded natural disaster, triggered by the second largest earthquake ever measured on a seismograph.

The Aegean was still that winter evening on Kalymnos, Greece, when I heard the news. I looked out at the darkened beach. Lanterns and shadows appeared as the local men set out to night-fish in small boats.

I suddenly understood what Mr Gurung had been trying to tell me with his big smile, the morning when I asked him about the shark: 'Yes, I know. I know what it means to be taken by the sea. To be consumed by her. And to escape from her, to find a way back to shore. To be a voyager between worlds.'

I don't know what happened to Mr Gurung when the tsunami hit. I hope he was out fishing.

If he was, I'm certain he's still alive.

David Pickford on the first ascent of the second (crux) pitch of *Wall of Spirits* (E8 6b) at Pentire Head, Cornwall, England. I returned in June 2006 with Sarah Garnett to add the first pitch (E6 6a) and complete the climb. The route still awaits both a continuous ascent and an onsight ascent.

September 2004

photo I Mike Robertson

Chris Doyle attempting the line that would become *The Brute* (8b), The Diamond, Little Orme, Llandudno, North Wales. The route saw many attempts by good climbers until finally falling to local strongman Neil Dyer in 2011. The Diamond is one of Britain's most exciting places for sea cliff sport climbing: it is extremely tidal, condition-dependent, and always comes served with seagulls. These factors combine to make a good day at the Diamond something really special.

August 2010

David Pickford bouldering at Capo Testa, the northern point of Sardinia, Italy

May 2005

photo I Sarah Garnett

Sarah Garnett bouldering on the sculpted granite of Capo Testa, Sardinia. The southern coast of neighbouring Corsica is visible on the horizon.

May 2006

From Russia With Love

War Games in Kyrgyzstan's Wild West

Sam Whittaker seconding pitch 3 on the first ascent of *From Russia With Love*
(E7 6b / ABO, 500m), Ak Su Valley, Kyrgyzstan

July 2005

At five past four in the morning the ancient Aeroflot Tupolov smashes into the runway at Manas airport. There is an audible intake of breath from the passengers as overhead lockers spring open, spewing their contents across the cabin floor. The plane is filled with a cacophony of creaking hinges, interspersed with other, less identifiable noises, culminating in a tremendous growl from the bowels of the fuselage. The aircrew look on, unflinching: it's clearly a perfectly normal landing. A great cheer rises from the back and curls like a gust of wind through the plane. The trio of Poles in the row behind me are in high spirits. They've been drinking vodka with kamikaze determination throughout the flight, and now propose a new round of toasts:

'To zee great nation of Poland! To zee exzellent Russian Kapitan! To ze great nation of Russia! To ze Republik of Kyrgyzstan! Okrzyki!' Their words slur into cheers and I smile at the post-Soviet solidarities. Mikhail Gorbachev would have surely been proud of our welcome to Kyrgyzstan.

As pre-dawn arrivals go, this was an unconventional one. We shamble out into the hush of the arrivals hall chattering loudly, like the after-party crowd leaving a nightclub at closing time, and whisk through immigration with the vodka fumes from the Poles building behind us. The revelry continues. Sam and Mark head for an empty bar with die-hard determination. Having woken the bartender, who had been snoring on his chair with an empty vodka bottle in one hand, they return with several beers. Too tired to stomach anything other than water, I crash out under the table to the sound of their chinking glasses. The hum of a distant vacuum in the terminal building lulls me into sleep.

I awake to the sound of a gigantic hoover scooping across the floor beside my table. Peering up, I am momentarily unsure whether my dream has ended, as I see that the man controlling the hoover massively dwarfs the enormous contraption itself.

Five hours later we drift out of the terminal and into the heat of the day. High summer on the steppes of Central Asia is often defined by a fervid haze that begins mid-morning and lasts well into the evening. The heavy air of Bishkek, capital of the Republic of Kyrgyzstan, hangs a few centimetres above the asphalt and shakes.

In the domestic airport, we find the Twin Otter at last in the far corner of the runway. I seek shade under one of the wings and notice a well-translated bit of Cyrillic plastered on the fuselage: 'Chop here with Crash Axe'. Reaching into my pack for a camera, a military policeman with the physique of a medium-sized adult gorilla starts to walk in my direction. As my camera appears, Rambo gently raises his Kalashnikov. Momentarily forgetting the Russian for 'terribly sorry, old chap', I stash the SLR out of sight. Rambo then howls with laughter, revealing a finely-polished set of glittering, metallic teeth. Gold teeth are a hallmark of status in Kyrgyzstan and its neighbouring countries, a sort of Central Asian equivalent of a top-of-the-range BMW.

We are bound for Osh, the main town on the Kyrgyz side of the Fergana Corridor, a long strip of fertile land that stretches west towards Samarkand and on to the deserts of Uzbekistan and Turkmenistan. Looking out of the window of the little plane as it begins its descent, the Pamir Alay rises sharply to the south. An immense wall of jagged spires and glinting white summits lifts out of the plains, defining the point where the steppe of Central Asia rises to meet the far western end of the Greater Himalaya. Two days later Ian [Parnell] arrives in Osh, having flown indirectly via London on his way back from climbing Everest. The team was now complete: Sam [Whittaker], Zippy [Mark Pretty], Grimer [Niall Grimes], Donie [O'Sullivan], Ian, and myself – or the 'Kyrgyz Six' as we would later call ourselves.

We are to leave for Ozgouruch next morning.

I wake at dawn to the drift of the call to prayer from the mosque across the street. We breakfast on black Kyrgyz eggs and strong black tea. The tea is always black and always strong in this country, and the men seem to drink it constantly. One local proverb goes 'If he does not drink tea, a Kyrgyz man will die'. In the eerie half-light, slurping our tea, we hear the approach of the Beast. Several minutes elapse, though, between the first sound of the approaching contraption and its tremendous arrival. With a demonic puff of foul smoke – an exotic mixture of diesel and other, more obscure petrochemicals – a fearsome vehicle we would christen 'The Beast' scowls into the yard.

Best described as a mechanical rhinoceros with extra sound effects, the remarkable 'Uuaz' is one of the engineering hallmarks of the former USSR where it provided a universal form of people-carrier from the Ukraine to Ulaanbaatar. With a flash of gold teeth in the dawn light, our driver appears behind The Beast's enormous wheel. He speaks almost no English but has a gentle, determined manner that instils confidence. Quickly he becomes known as 'Shortcut'. His Kyrgyz name sounds almost identical to the English word, and, more to the point, it sounds good. If anyone can get us across 400 miles of potholed desert roads and through several military checkpoints in this unlikely contraption, Shortcut is the man.

The Beast's starter-motor erupts with the noise of a squadron of MiG-28s on take-off and we hit the road west towards Ozgouruch, the tiny village at the road head to Karavshin.

Less than an hour out of Osh, though, The Beast grinds to a halt.

'Is there a problem, Shortcut?' I enquire.

'No problem. I fix. Ten minute.'

Shortcut looks unperturbed. After 10 minutes of fiddling with the engine, he establishes the fault – a broken distributor arm – and ingeniously but optimistically attempts to fix it with part of a baked bean can. Firing up the engine again, The Beast revolts at his repair and spits out the entire assembly in an explosion of bolts and fragments of tin. Our prospects of reaching Ozgouruch today are not looking good. Shortcut merely shrugs, wanders across the dusty highway and hitches a ride with a truck back to Osh to find a replacement part.

A sand-coloured sun rises over Fergana to the east as the dust-cloud of the truck disappears. We play football in the road as the chill of dawn fades with the creeping heat of the morning. After a while, another dust-cloud appears in the distance and a battered Lada rolls to a halt. Our unflappable driver swings out of the Lada wielding a new distributor cap which he bolts on, a cigarette dangling precariously out of his mouth over the oil-caked engine. He turns the enormous crank and The Beast belches into life with a renewed vigour. In the burning midday heat we lurch down an endless road through a desert full of gigantic potholes. At an unmarked crossroads, two bored Kyrgyz soldiers emerge from a checkpoint steaming with vodka fumes, bristling with weaponry, and asking for our passports with a languid curiosity. Clearly mystified by our presence, they wave us on, making a vague gesture of their AK47s towards the mountains to the south.

It is almost dark as we reach Isfara. Children are playing in the dusty street, wide eyes flashing with the light from roadside fires. At the edge of the small town we turn south again, then west towards the castellated dusk sky. From here, the road curls tortuously up a steep valley towards Ozgouruch. Just before midnight, as we cross a bridge of recycled wooden railway sleepers, I hear the Kara Su river roaring through the darkness below. A blast of icy air hits me as I open The Beast's rear window, craning my head. Far above, the ridgeline is in strong silhouette against a night sky dense with stars. Further to the south, the snowy peaks of the Kara Su valley dim the star-sheen slightly. The two hundred mile journey from Osh has taken 19 hours.

Nothing you might have heard about Karavshin, a remote village deep in the mountains of south western Kyrgyzstan, will prepare you for the feeling of arriving there. With tired legs after two days of hard walking we emerge from the arid lower canyon onto high pasture. A short way ahead of our horsemen, we stop beyond some mud-brick houses at a small clearing among stunted pines where the glacial Ak Su river levels on to a gravel flood plain. It is almost dusk and a cold wind is blowing off the high mountains to the south, from Tajikistan. Through the trees, three immense shapes begin to define the western rim of the valley while to the east loom another two monolithic summits. We set up base camp as night gathers among the boulders under Central Pyramid, its monumental outline cut sharp against the night sky of the Pamir Alay.

After a few days of unstable weather the sky clears one evening after a thunderstorm, promising a change. Sam and I have set our hopes on a slender, unclimbed pillar rising out of the back of the massive couloir between Central Pyramid and the Russian Tower. We fall into a restless sleep with fingers crossed, daunted and intrigued by the forthcoming challenge.

A chill wind engulfs the mountains about us. A massive slab kicks back at me as I fight the interminable creep of my rock-shoes on its tiny crystals. Climbing gear swings about my harness, useless. There is no protection. I must decide to move. I move. The sky overhead turns dark. The sound of rushing cloud fills my ears.

I wake in the icy chill before dawn, peering out of the tent to see the early light catching the three summits to the west. The air is cold and still, the morning sky an inky, polarised blue.

'Hey Sam, you awake?'

A furtive reply comes from the depths of his sleeping bag.

'Looks like it's settled.'

A local hunter who stayed with us last night has rekindled the fire and is squatting in front of it, warming his hands, breaking sticks for kindling. We gulp down tea with a few pieces of indigestible flatbread before beginning the steep ascent across the scree-cones under the enormous bulk of Central Pyramid. An hour later, we're gearing up at the head of the couloir. Sam sets off up a slabby rake from which the great pillar rises. He climbs quickly across initial slabs of lichenous granite. As he arranges a belay, I get a chance to take in where I am.

The sun is still hidden behind the icy bulk of the Russian Tower's north wall. The silence of the couloir is shattered intermittently as huge chunks of ice and rock peel away from the wall and plunge more than a thousand feet to the screes. From the safe distance of our position

Morning cloud swirls around the Russian Tower, Ak Su Valley, Kyrygzstan

July 2005

on the pillar I watch the tumbling debris with an alarmed fascination. Occasional chill gusts eddy around the couloir; a pair of Lammergeiers circle on an early thermal coming off the moraine under Wolf Peak.

'Okay Dave, when you're ready.' Sam's voice brings me back to the rock and the challenge in wait above us. I follow the pitch slowly, kicking my toes against the granite crystals, trying to get the blood back in my feet. By the time I arrive at the belay the sun has just swung over the Russian Tower and we shed thermals, enjoying the warmth. Above our marginal stance soars a perfect open groove, disappearing just before the arête that bounds the right hand edge of the pillar. We swing leads and I climb on into the groove. All too soon, after sixty metres of immaculate climbing on equally perfect granite, Sam warns that I've run out of rope. Above, the groove vanishes in about 10 metres and is capped by a series of daunting overlaps. Sam leads on through, eager to get on with the climbing. Moving out right from the top of the groove, his progress slows, eventually coming to a halt at a final overlap. 'How does it look?' I enquire.

'There's a sea of granite up here Dave, I don't think it'll go this way.'

There is an audible silence. I think we are both weighing up exactly how disappointing a retreat would be from this point.

'How about reversing back to the groove and breaking out left around the arête?' I suggest from the security of the belay.

Sam arrives back at the top of the groove, the slack already looping out on his right rope, the way ahead uncertain. After a while, he chalks up, cleans his boots and makes a delicate, precise move out left on to the arête. I can hear him breathing with those brief, deep exhalations that say far more than any words can about the gravity of a climb. After another short pause, he says with a quiet assurance: 'Ok, watch me, I'm going for it.' Then he disappears around the arête and out of my field of vision.

The ropes inch out. Vagrant gusts come and go, blowing chill air from the shadows of the icy couloir to the right. When the air is still I can feel the warmth of a thermal rising from the open slabs way beneath us. Occasionally there is a hollow boom from the depths of the couloir as another massive chunk of ice and granite explodes into the scree. Then suddenly there is a different sound from high to my left – a brief shout of adrenaline release, and relief.

I detect the urgency of his movements as the ropes pull out quickly, pause for a second, inch back, pull out again, inch back, stop. After an indeterminate moment, they haul out firmly for another metre. As I hear Sam's holler of success I feel my own nerves settle. Instinctively knowing the meaning of his exclamation, I shout an enthusiastic reply into the wind.

And all too soon I'm above the groove, back-stepping through those wretched overlaps. I remove the final, small cam Sam has placed high on the right rope with trepidation, watching it loop, slack and useless across the wall to the left. I guess it must be at least 20 metres to the side runner above Sam's belay. Switching off, I reverse the intricate moves back to the groove, soon peering around the arête with some relief. A faint line of chalk weaves across a featureless slab to Sam's belay in a tiny niche 15 metres to the left. He beams across at me.

'That was the hardest bit of onsight climbing I've ever done.'

With rather less enthusiasm, I'm calculating the length of a potential pendulum. I'm precariously balanced on minute footholds and although not quite as dangerous as on the lead, a fall from here would take me on an extensive sideways tour of the abyss below.

Eventually, I get the better of the weight of my camera and the monster pendulum yawning back at me, and make a series of intricate moves left to a rest on a tiny edge. Part of it crumbles away and I stab my foot back at it, holding on friction. Sam laughs. I look up left, smiling with incredulity at the seriousness of the pitch. Safer now, having closed the angle to the last gear considerably, I enjoy a brilliant final sequence to the belay.

After a while, I set off up the daunting crack-line in the impending wall above us. I move strenuously through wild terrain, studiously avoiding a giant, booming flake somehow welded to the retaining wall. Pulling through the last of a series of small but awkward overhangs, I find a secure belay, content in the knowledge that we have finally unlocked the puzzle of one of the most perfect and elegant lines either of us have ever seen. Sam soon appears around the roof, his grin even wider now, and races on up the easier angled continuation of the crack.

After another massive pitch, I belay on the apex of the pillar. We revel in our new perspective on the surrounding world of towering granite walls and snow-capped peaks, sharply etched by the late afternoon sunlight at 4500 metres. Eventually, we find the top of a reasonable-looking abseil line down an enormous dihedral system we'd spotted from below. Halfway down, the evening shadows race up from the couloir to overtake us.

Only a few hundred feet from the scree and we look back up at the line. The last sunlight falls across the pillar, just discernible among the deep shadows of the couloir, a slender orange brush-stroke against the vast, darkening wall. Pulling the ropes on the final abseil, we watch and remain silent. That last moment of light captures everything we might have said then, about why we had chosen to make the long journey to Ak Su, or why we ever go climbing.

Top to bottom: Central Pyramid (left) and The Russian Tower (right) standing proud above the meadows of the upper Ak Su valley. The line taken by *From Russia With Love* follows the slender pillar just to the left of the main monolith of The Russian Tower. | A local woman making flatbread in her yurt in Karavshin, the tiny village at the entrance to the Ak Su valley. | The map of the Karavshin region: no less than 4 countries all connect at this point: Krygyzstan, Uzbekistan, Tajikistan and Kazakhstan. The region is a diverse cultural and ethnic melting pot and a hotbed of political instability. | A Krygyz soldier rests in a makeshift fortification in the lower Ak Su valley, which was the scene of fierce fighting in 1999 during which the well-known American climbers Tommy Caldwell and Beth Rodden were kidnapped by insurgents. They later slipped capture and escaped.

Left to right: Sam Whittaker silhouetted against the Pamir Alay near the top of *From Russian With Love* on the first ascent. | Sam Whittaker and David Pickford working hard on diplomacy in the Ak Su Valley at the time of their arrest. | Sam Whittaker seconding pitch 8 on the first ascent of *From Russia With Love*. | The bustling Osh Bazaar. | Our Soviet-era Uuaz, aka 'The Beast', resting against a small tree in Ozgouruch after our driver, Shortcut, made a somewhat over-ambitious reversing manoeuvre. Ian Parnell is in the passenger's seat, looking down at the raging river twenty metres below him. We managed to rescue both the Beast and Ian from their near-drowning experience using climbing ropes, logs, and manpower.

July 2005

At dawn, from somewhere down the valley, comes the crack of a Kalashnikov, probably fired by those half-trained, half-mad Kyrgyz soldiers from Batken. The soldiers arrive and we find we are leaving Ak Su under a very Russian kind of 'unofficial arrest'. We have no permit, they tell us. Where is our permit? Yes, we reply. We tried many times to get one, but you cannot get one in Batken.

Thirty-six hours later I'm in a small cell in the army barracks in Batken with two Kyrgyz officials cross-examining me in a mixture of Russian and Kyrygz. The fat man on the right calls himself 'The General'. The skinny one – who looks, talks, and smells like he's had a few too many vodkas already – calls himself 'Mister Zulu'. A few English phrases, of course, are thrown in for good measure.

It is like being a contestant in a Russian version of *I'm A Celebrity Get Me Out Of Here* with a reference to Tarantino's *Reservoir Dogs*. The General and Mister Zulu are playing good-cop-bad-cop, but cannot decide which of them is which. Like a couple of teenage boys desperate to impress, they carry on until the absurdity of the situation slowly dawns on them. Mister Zulu slinks off for his vodka and The General opens the door, suddenly assuming an air of military seriousness:

'So you may tell zur frientz zat maybe you stay in zis platz for some days.'

I break the news to the others, my throat parched from the dry air and The General's cigarette smoke. In need of refreshment, I go over the road to where a small boy has arrived on an enormous bicycle laden with watermelons. Biting into a slice, I walk back to pass the melon round to the others. They are convulsed with laughter.

'What is it Sam?' I ask. Turning back towards the barracks, I see Mister Zulu greedily knocking back another shot by the main gateway.

'Now they… they want a couple of hundred som for more vodka…!'

Hours later, we are rattling back across the featureless desert on the Uzbek border when Shortcut pronounces he is lost.

'How can we possibly be lost?' Grimer enquires, to a murmur of agreement. It is nearly midnight and we are all knackered. Shortcut has stopped his interminable chain smoking, so even he must be in need of a break. We shamble out of The Beast and crash out instantly on the sand.

Twenty-six hours after leaving Batken, we arrive back in Osh at mid-afternoon and bid goodbye to Shortcut, tipping him handsomely for getting us to and from Ozgouruch in such style. He departs with his signature flash of gold teeth. That evening, I read the news on the internet. A couple of weeks have passed since the 7 July bombings in London. In no mood for sleep after everyone else has retired, I stay up reading. After a while, I hear a woman's voice beyond the curtain separating the courtyard from the house. It is Ury's wife, beginning her late reading of the Koran in its original ancient Arabic. It is unusual to hear women reading the language. Her voice is clear and sharp, lifting and falling through the air like windblown snow. It sounds like the voice of a woman far younger. Fig leaves rustle in the empty courtyard and the vines rattle in the desert wind overhead. The night air smells of dust and wood-smoke. Suddenly, the woman's voice rises in crescendo, and with a final 'Allahu Akbar' falls silent.

Another gust of wind blows through the fig tree, colder now, stiffening the quiet courtyard with the nightmarish reality of contemporary history. To me, this Kyrgyz woman's hauntingly beautiful reading of the Koran now seems as an elegy – an elegy for the Americans who died on September 11th 2001, the British and American servicemen killed in Iraq and Afghanistan, for the countless Iraqi civilians who have died since 2003, and for the Londoners blown up just two weeks ago.

Two days later, we're back in Bishkek. After the wildness of the Pamir and the wild-west characters of Karavshin there is a certain refreshing austerity to the glum Soviet blocks and monolithic heaps of concrete masquerading as public art that line the streets of the capital. Cities are odd places after several weeks in the high mountains of Asia.

It is 4.15 a.m. and the hatchet-faced Russian clerk at the Aeroflot check-in desk wants money. She is trying to weigh our baggage and all manoeuvres to try and divert her prove ineffective. Even the two bottles of vodka I produce as a goodwill gesture fail to register. Ian is convulsed with hysterical laughter as we wait to board our plane to Moscow, completely stripped of our last reserves of cash but happy to have made our great escape from Kyrgyzstan, the Batken barracks, the vodka fumes of Mister Zulu, and the ire of The General.

Just before we taxi away to take off, at the back of the plane the door swings open and in strides a uniformed official.

'Are zer six Engliz Alpinistz on zeez airkraft?' he barks repeatedly in the tone of a disgruntled bullmastiff as he strides down the cabin.

'Shit' Zippy breathes through clenched teeth.

Sam's eyes roll with anxiety and sleep deprivation. Donie and Grimer left on an earlier flight, so at least there aren't six of us. Zippy, Ian and Sam have their hand baggage checked for climbing gear, which, fortunately, they are not carrying.

'Alpinists?' Zippy asks with a confused expression.

'No, no, we're just tourists,' Ian chips in immediately.

'We have just been on holiday in your excellent country,' adds Sam.

Lacking the linguistic ability to contest our explanation, the official nods slowly in evident disappointment. After a while, he turns around with the painful expression of a man who has just lost a game of high stakes poker, and walks back towards the door of the plane. The grins widen as the cabin doors close, and we burst into paroxysmal laughter.

'The Kyrgyz Six!' Zippy proclaims triumphantly.

'Long live the Kyrgyz Six!' Sam replies.

The voices of my friends fade as the engines roar into life, and I'm pulled back into my seat as the decrepit Tupolev lifts into the summer night. I watch the lights of Bishkek fade below until they vanish altogether. Leaning back against the window, I am overcome by waves of sleep.

A chill wind engulfs the mountains about us. The sky overhead turns dark. The sound of rushing cloud fills my ears.

This account of the first ascent of From Russia With Love *by Sam Whittaker and David Pickford (500m, E7 6b / 5.12 X / ABO), Ak Su Valley, Kyrgyzstan, in July 2005 was first published in* The Alpine Journal.

Charlie Woodburn on the second pitch of *Call of the Sea* (E3 5c, 95 metres) on the west face of Dun Mingulay, Mingulay Island, Outer Hebrides, Scotland

June 2008

Crusoe & The Witch

56° 48' 41.39" North, 7° 38' 15.04" West

The air over Guarsay Mor turns with shadows as we approach. They dart and wheel like huge bats through a darkening sky. Then a sudden rush of displaced air hits Charlie and me, almost simultaneously, from a blindspot on the left. Two of these vicious terrordactyls swoop so low their spiny feet skim our ears.

'What the hell was that?' Charlie spins around, blinking into the sky as another pair set their sights on us with swept-back wings.

'Bonxies!' Garth exclaims. 'Keep to the ridge, away from the nests.'

'Aaarrrggghhh' erupts from Neil as another attacker sweeps in, and we make haste for the sanctuary of the clifftop.

We're on the uninhabited island of Mingulay at the southern extremity of Scotland's Outer Hebrides. It lies some twelve miles southwest of Barra, the nearest inhabited place. It's one of the most remote of all the British islands. Although continuously inhabited for around two thousand years, evacuations began in 1907 and by 1912 the island had been completely abandoned by its human residents. As with the even more remote St Kilda, there were numerous reasons for the evacuation. It seems likely that the sheer hardship of life on the island – particularly during winter when it became inaccessible for months at a time – was a major factor in the final exodus, when the prospect of an easier life on the larger islands to the north became possible.

Through the rest of the twentieth century, Mingulay was mainly left alone to its resident populations of razorbills, guillemots, kittiwakes, and puffins. It was not until the early 1990's that climbers discovered the Lewisean Gneiss crags surrounding the island that would harbour some of the most spectacular sea cliff climbing in Britain. The igneous rock of Mingulay is part of one of the earth's oldest geological groups: it was already four hundred million years old when the Himalayas were being formed. As you'd think given its antiquity, it is generally extremely solid, with gritstone-like friction and frequent opportunities to place natural protection. The first recorded routes on Mingulay were climbed by Mick Fowler and Chris Bonington, a partnership that indicates climbing of a highly adventurous nature was to be found here. New climbs have been pioneered by a handful of visitors every summer from 1995 onwards, and the hundred-metre northwest wall of Dun Mingulay, an imposing promontory that harbours the remains of an Iron Age fort, is now regarded as one of Britain's best.

The idea of sailing to Mingulay from the Scottish mainland came about through a plan hatched on Lundy – that other showpiece of offshore British climbing. But how exactly do you get five climbers with the collective nautical experience of a toad across ninety miles of the most treacherous inshore waters in Britain?

Enter Patrick Trust, our very own Captain Ahab, skipper of Hecate. Patrick has sailed the turbulent channel that separates the Inner and Outer Hebrides for close to fifty years. The plan was simple: we would sail out to Mingulay from Ardfern on Loch Craignish, where Patrick would leave us to make course north for Barra, Eriskay and Harris, returning in a week's time.

The voyage out on midsummer's night couldn't have been better timed, as our departure coincided with a ridge of high pressure over northwest Scotland. The Sound of Jura was almost flat calm as we turned Craignish Point, and the ink-dark water sluiced under the hull. The perfect sea conditions were fortunate, since our plan was to make a short cut out into the Firth of Lorn through the notorious Gulf of Corryvreckan. This narrow stretch of water separating the Isle of Jura from Scarba is one of the most turbulent stretches of inshore water in the northern hemisphere. Formerly classified as 'unnavigable', the Admiralty's *West Coast of Scotland Pilot's Guide To Inshore Waters* still calls it 'very violent and dangerous' and says 'no vessel should attempt this passage without local knowledge'. In certain conditions, the world's third largest tidal whirlpool forms here above a submerged rock pinnacle. Even on the quiet night on which we sailed, standing waves almost a metre high formed at Corryvreckan's seaward reach. The sun rose as we passed through the Sound of Iona off the western tip of Mull at around four a.m., and we headed out into the Minch on a perfect summer's morning.

The panorama that now lay before us was enough to put any thoughts of seasickness at bay. A chain of blue-green islands lazed on an idle sea to the west. Barra to the north, then Vatersay and Sandray; Pabbay lay a little closer still, and then on our course at dead reckoning, Mingulay.

We dropped anchor off the sandy beach on the east coast, one of only two landing spots on the island. After a delicious slap-up lunch of shepherd's pie on the aft deck, we had work to do.

The dinghy was launched and after at least a dozen runs to shore and back, we'd landed our gargantuan stash of kit and food on the beach with no need, remarkably, to jettison anything. Our skipper, Patrick, rowed back out to Hecate and pulled her anchor, giving us a final wave as he motored out, finally disappearing around the point to the north, bound for the sheltered sanctuary of Castlebay on Barra. Finally, we were the castaways on Mingulay we'd first imagined in the smoky back room of Lundy's Marisco Tavern almost two years ago.

The fallout of a deep Atlantic low pressure system strikes Mingulay's exposed, east-facing beach and the island's only landing place. The island was inhabited until 1912, and its residents would have been completely cut off from neighbouring islands Pabbay and Barra for long periods due to high seas.

June 2008

Neil Gresham leads the first pitch up the sweeping wall of *Ray of Light* (E4 6a, 110 metres) on the awesome west face of Dun Mingulay, Mingulay Island, Outer Hebrides, Scotland. One of the most impressive sea cliffs in the UK, this wall is home to dozens of three star extremes between E2 and E7.

June 2008

Simon Tappin climbing the thin finger crack of *A Word With The Bill* (E3 5c) on the west face of Guarsay Mor, Mingulay, on our first reconnaissance of the island.

June 2008

Tents were quickly pitched, and before long we'd shouldered packs and climbed to the wide col on the ridge that forms the undulating spine of the island. Dodging the dreaded Bonxies on the higher slopes of Guarsay Mor, we eventually made it down to the clifftop. Despite the ominous signs of a front pressing in, with streams of cirrus darkening and building across the sky to the south, we managed to get a couple of climbs in that evening.

Sunday dawned grey and chilly as the full force of a northerly gale began to make its presence felt. An old Scottish myth tells that the hag goddess of winter, Cailleach Bheur, uses the Gulf of Corryvreckan to wash her plaid, and this then ushers the turn of the seasons from autumn to winter. I hoped we hadn't stirred her from her summer sleep on Friday night as we crossed the Gulf. Hecate, after all, is a ringleader of witches in European mythology. Casting spurious thoughts of witchcraft aside over another round of fresh coffee, we put the poor conditions to our advantage and made a reconnaissance of the northern half of the island.

That night the weather cleared, and tomorrow's sights were set on the great precipice of Dun Mingulay, reportedly the island's best climbable cliff. Sure enough, the next morning was fine and breakfast quickly merged into the organisation of gear and ropes, and we struck up the hill to the south west. To gain the promontory of Sron An Duin you must cross a narrow col, and the view down into the chasm below is truly awe-inspiring: the eye plummets more than four hundred feet into a dark cauldron filled with circling gulls.

Throwing the entire length of a hundred metre static line out over a sea cliff is a relatively rare experience; there are few crags in Britain that require more than three hundred feet of abseiling to reach their base. Most of them, like Carn Gowla's America Buttress, are fabled for their imposing grandeur and for the committing nature of their climbs.

Dun Mingulay is certainly no exception to this rule.

The crag was still wrapped in the morning's shadow. Beyond the point gannets dived for fish, falling like thrown spears into the sea. Seals welcomed us with their familiar inquisitions, appearing and vanishing, then reappearing even closer to shore. Even in such calm conditions, a slow Atlantic groundswell sucked along the base of the cliff, reminding us that the next dry land to the west would be the beaches of Nova Scotia or the cliffs of Newfoundland.

It was a perfect day to be here. Just as I topped out on the spectacular forty-five metre final pitch of *Call of the Sea*, the sun swung round and lit up the entire northwest wall of Dun Mingulay. Veins of quartz suddenly sparked like silver fish in the rising light.

By six o'clock the tide was low and with another six hours of light

to play with we moved the rope over to the huge arch at the centre of Sron An Duin, home to the most impressive climbs on the island. As I belayed the others on the superb second roof pitch of *The Great Shark Hunt* (E4 5c) a Minke whale surfaced for air just beyond the point, and the evening sun glistened off its back before it plunged again into the deep. I watched Neil making steady progress up the final pitch of *Ray of Light* (E4 6a) where some of the holds stick out like gigantic tusks almost a metre from the main wall. As we sorted gear and coiled ropes that evening, still blessed with sunlight at ten o'clock, we found it difficult to come to terms with just how good the climbing here really was. Walking back over the hill, St Kilda, the most remote of all the British islands, appeared unmistakably on the northwest horizon.

The weather report crackled on the VHF radio early on Tuesday morning, and the possibility of being stranded on the island dawned: *This is Clyde Coastguard. There are gale warnings in force for Rockall, Malin, Hebrides… Now the general situation at 0900 hours. Ardnamurchan Point including the Outer Hebrides: easterly gale force 8, backing south easterly and increasing severe gale 9, imminent. Rain then showers. Sea state: very rough or high.*

That night we were battered by the full force of that easterly gale howling off The Minch, and the double-overhead surf breaking on the beach didn't make our prospects of escape look any better. Luckily, the wind swung around to the south west and settled to a more reasonable level on Thursday, and when we woke on Friday – the date of our intended departure – the sea was as calm as when we arrived. I scanned the murky horizon for signs of a mast. As our final supplies of fresh coffee bubbled in the percolator, a familiar voice came in on the radio: *Mingulay, Mingulay, Mingulay. This is yacht Hecate. Do you read me? Over.*

Our captain had weathered some of the worst June storms in recent memory and had made it down to collect us in perfect time. A muted cheer drifted over the beach as Hecate appeared through the mist. There was a mingled sense of relief at catching the weather-lull and sadness at having to leave the island. A couple of hours out into the Minch, a pod of bottlenose dolphins joined us, diving across the bow and plunging under the hull for almost an hour, leaving us enchanted by their free companionship.

That evening, we waited for the flood tide in Tobermory's sheltered harbour at the northern entrance to the Sound of Mull. Standing with shaky legs on inhabited land for the first time in a week, the wildness of Mingulay vividly returned as I looked out across the cinder sky over Ardnamurchan, knowing I'd have to set sail sometime again across that dolphin-torn sea.

Top: The Gulf of Corryvrecken or 'Cauldron of the Plaid', site of the world's third-largest tidal whirlpool, which the team sailed aboard the yacht Hecate en route for the Minch and Mingulay. Connoisseurs of literary history should note that the passage was first swum by the writer George Orwell's one-legged brother-in-law, Bill Dunn.
Centre: Charlie Woodburn makes landfall on the east beach of Mingulay – the island's only landing place. Yacht Hecate is anchored in the bay beyond.
Lower: A Bonxie attacks Mark Garthwaite and Simon Tappin on the high ground of Guarsay Mor, Mingulay. These birds are large, vociferous, highly aggressive, and will strike humans during their spring nesting season.

June 2008

Island in the Stream

51°10' 37.8876' North, 4°39' 57.96' West

Lundy is a place of interest to most people for being England's first statutory Marine Nature Reserve, for its endemic species of cabbage, and for its colourful history involving piracy, Ottoman occupation, and a crackpot one-man monarchist movement by Martin Coles Harman in the 1920s, which featured a new coinage system organised in denominations of 'Puffin' (he was fined five pounds and fifteen guineas by the House of Lords, but he kept his claim to being King). Some may have taken the time to make a brief visit. Yet to many climbers, the island of Lundy is not merely a three mile long by one mile wide piece of granite lying twelve miles off the north Devon coast. It is a way of life. Every year, mainly in August and September due to the widespread nesting restrictions, a small-scale exodus takes place within the British climbing community to the west coast of Lundy.

In August and September 2007 – one of the most prolific climbing seasons the island has ever seen – Paul Harrison put the final notes and new routes into the text of the 2008 guidebook and numerous teams descended on the cliffs during an Indian summer that lasted into October.

Around five hundred years ago, Shakespeare described England as a 'precious stone set in a silver sea…' (Richard II). His words sound a long way removed from the urbanised, overpopulated country we live in today. But the place eulogised by John of Gaunt does still exist, and finds its modern counterpart and continuity on places like Lundy Island.

A friend of mine described his sense, after a first trip to the island, that 'it captures all the best things about England – a unique landscape, a strong community – and a great pub.'

To cap it off, some of the best granite sea cliff climbing in the world is to be found on Lundy. If it sounds like a fairytale to you and too good to be true, just get hold of a copy of Paul Harrison's guidebook and take a look for yourself.

The swell gurgles among the boulders, slurping into the depths of a chasm extending into the bowels of the island. Tim and I are lashed to a tiny triangular ledge by an assortment of microwires beneath a wall that leers down at us for three hundred feet overhead. For reasons which at this point are not entirely clear, I set off into a void of inhospitable, unclimbed rock, up a line of cracks ending in an acutely overhanging groove bisecting a roof about twenty metres above the stance.

Tim spied the line a few days ago. It's an awesome sheet of vertical granite seamed by spidery cracks rising the full height of the north wall of Deep Zawn, to the right of Pat Littlejohn's classic *Antiworlds*. Yesterday, putting optimism before discretion, I abbed down into the void with the imminent onset of a thunderstorm snarling at me from the west. Bouncing around on the end of a three hundred foot rope, like a string puppet playing a charade with the tempest, I attempted to sketch a possible way through the overhangs splitting the right-hand side of the zawn. But the weather held sway, and I jumared out with the first fat drops of a late summer downpour bouncing off my helmet. Packing my gear in the sheeting rain, I admitted to Tim that I, too, had been captivated by the drama of the wall, and the challenge of the line.

Back in the depths of the zawn the next morning, I'm setting off up the first pitch, shoving cams into a booming, inverted tooth of granite hanging from the roof, like a vampiric fang awaiting its first blood.

My left hand suddenly flies out of the flake as my jam disintegrates, and I almost cartwheel out of balance. Somehow regaining composure, I manage to stab my left foot out into a wild bridge on the very lip of the roof as a trickle of dark blood draws patterns across my forearm. I throw another cam in, trying to ignore the daunting hollow boom of the flakes, and concentrate on the sequence: the security of the *Antiworlds* stance is transformed from a mirage into a welcome relief.

We're one down, and one to go.

Tim Emmett leading the second and crux pitch of *The Fifth Ace* (E6 6b, 6b) at Deep Zawn, Lundy Island, on the first ascent in August 2005. The name of the route derives from the poem 'Antiworlds and The Fifth Ace' by the contemporary Russian poet Andrey Voznesensky. The route immediately to the left, *Antiworlds*, is the classic of the zawn and one of the best E4's in the UK.

August 2005

photo | Simon Cardy

Neil Dickson making an onsight ascent of the very bold face climb *Mayan Skies* (E7 6b) at Black Crag, Old Light Area, Lundy Island, Bristol Channel, England

September 2007

Charlie Woodburn cruising the crux pitch of *Supernova* (E5 6b),
Deep Zawn, Lundy Island

August 2006

Johnny Woods (1976–2011) soaring high on *Voyage of the Acolyte* (E6 6b),
Two Legged Zawn, Lundy Island (photo | Hugo Glover)

August 2005   – rest in peace, my friend –

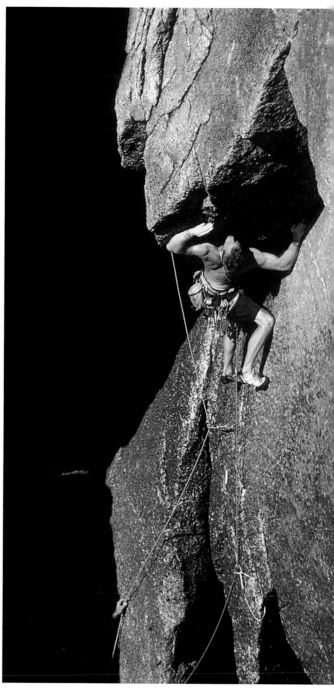

Charlie Woodburn making the first ascent of *Kullus* (E6 6c) at Flying
Buttress, Lundy Island

August 2005

Yesterday evening, Tim's all-guns-blazing onsight attempt was thwarted above the final roof. Once again, we jumared out of the zawn as the drizzle increased to what the Radio 4 Shipping Forecast – perhaps somewhat euphemistically – calls 'intermittent light rain'. Despite the weather closing in, we're hopeful of our last chance tomorrow before the boat home.

The morning of our last day on the island dawns fine and clear, promising perfect conditions on the headwall. A cool breeze is gusting in from the sea as we arrive back at the belay, and Tim sets off, once again, into that beckoning wilderness of vertical granite. This time he looks confident and relaxed as he steps into the long reach through the first roof. In the zawn's depths, the seals bark and howl. I pay out the rope, shouting encouragement as Tim makes the desperate stretch over the final roof. He throws in a good wire just as a particularly loquacious series of throaty honks echoes up from the boulders, and I grin at the thought that the seals are engaging in the spectacle too. Suddenly, an exclamation from above interrupts the seal songs. Finally, Tim has cracked it and *The Fifth Ace* is on the table.

After a while, I'm climbing through the roof and established on the intricate sequence on the headwall, marvelling at the route's perfect balance, poise and position. How could such a wild card have been left unturned for so long in the great game of poker that is Lundy climbing?

Watching the island slowly vanish in the summer haze from the deck of the Oldenburg that evening, I knew it wouldn't be too long before I'd be back gambling again.

Neil Gresham in mid-flight during one of several splashdowns before the first deep water solo ascent of *The Flying Dutchman* at Flying Buttress, Lundy Island

August 2006

Neil Gresham flying high as the sun goes down on the first deep water solo ascent of *The Flying Dutchman* (pitch 1, E7 / 7b+) Lundy Island

August 2006

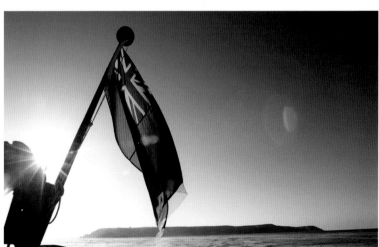

Sailing east for the English mainland, Lundy Island vanishes in the summer haze

August 2007

Bring on the Wall

Climbing in Madagascar's Tsaranoro Massif

We had been driving for sixteen hours straight when it started to rain. Huge thunderheads were building in the east and the night air crackled with electricity. We pulled over to tie tarpaulins over the luggage on the roof of the jeep.

'Good idea' our driver murmured in heavily accented French, and a wry smile spread across his face.

'To stop bandits!'

The four of us burst into laughter at the thought of a few tarpaulins fending off raiders, although we were more concerned about our crucial supplies of climbing rope and equipment getting soaked by the storm than the possibility of kidnap. Satisfied with the job, our driver lit another cigarette and started the engine. The rain drummed on the roof of the jeep like a jackhammer. As we rolled off into the night, a ten-second burst of sheet lightning illuminated the wild country to the west, and along the horizon to the south we could see the jagged shadow of a mountain range.

'It's over there!' Jack pointed into the maelstrom, as the lightning continued to spit fire across the jungle.

'Tsaranoro!'

I couldn't have expected a more dramatic first sight of the place that has become known to climbers across the world as 'the Yosemite of Africa'.

The climbing world is like a medieval court: messages of derring-do are relayed from distant lands, then passed around and discussed before the next quest. The idea of an exploratory rock climbing expedition to the mountains of southern Madagascar came about in early 2008, after Jack Geldard and I heard about the potential for establishing new routes there. We recruited James McHaffie – one of Britain's top climbers – and another friend, Stephen Horne, to make up a team of four. Preparations lasted several months, and we arrived on Madagascar at the beginning of April. We had one month to complete our main objectives: we wanted to establish a completely new climb, and attempt

the uncompleted project route called *Tough Enough* on a sheer fifteen-hundred foot monolith called Karimbony. This climb already had an almost mythical status among some of the world's best rock climbers. When completed, it would surely be the world's hardest big-wall free climb. Few routes in the world at that time had so many pitches of sustained and challenging rock climbing as the awesome West Face of Karimbony.

We arrived at Tsaranoro just before midnight, after a nineteen-hour journey south from the capital, Antananarivo. The electrical storm that had lit the final part of our journey had passed, and I lay in my sleeping bag and looked up at the shadow of the Tsaranoro Massif, towering thousands of feet above us. The stars were so bright it seemed they would burn holes in my mosquito net. It felt incredible to be here at last, in the heart of one of Africa's most exciting climbing areas.

After making ascents of some established routes to get used to the subtropical heat, we went in search of an unclimbed cliff where we could create our new route. After a day of trekking around the massif, cutting new trails and scoping the crags with binoculars, we found a perfect, natural climbing line on a cliff called Lemur Wall (so named because the endemic Madagascan primates, the Lemurs, populate the jungle at the base). It stretched up for around six hundred feet, following a striking yellow streak in the black granite. Like skiers looking down a couloir of pristine champagne powder, we knew this one was going to be awesome.

During our first day on the route, Jack and I established the first pitch, with a view to free climbing it after we had practised the moves. This initial section of the wall seemed to be the hardest, involving some very difficult climbing on microscopic holds. We tried to free climb it the next day, but failed due to the mercilessly rough rock and hot conditions. That night at base camp, I suggested that we needed an alternative approach to the main challenge of the line, in case we couldn't free climb the desperately hard first pitch.

Back up at our advance base camp under the wall, I looked at the rock on either side of the very difficult first section with an open-minded approach. The wall to the left seemed even more blank and impossible than what we'd been trying to climb. Jack and I looked up at it, and defeat seemed to stare back us. But then I had a brainwave. To the right, a gigantic vine hung down the side of a dank, overhanging gully. If we climbed it, I worked out that we could probably make a traverse out to a point just above the 'impossible' lower section of the wall. I placed a bolt for protection then made the leap of faith and grabbed the vine, swinging out on it and then climbing, Tarzan-style, to a tiny ledge about forty feet up. Amazingly, it didn't snap, much to Jack's disappointment. (Climbers have a natural tendency towards schadenfreude in such situations.)

One of the tiny crystal edges typical of much of the climbing on *Tough Enough* (8b+, 380 metres) on the west face of Karimbony, Tsaranoro Massif, Madagascar.

April 2008

James McHaffie on pitch 8 of the awesome *Tough Enough* (8b+, 380 metres) on the west face of Karimbony, Tsaranoro Massif, Madagascar. McHaffie and David Pickford free climbed five pitches of the line in spring 2008. It was later free climbed in its entirety (in 8 pitches) by a French team led by Arnaud Petit in autumn 2008. Czech superstar Adam Ondra then made an amazing onsight ascent of the climb, aged 17, in a single day in 2009. The route is among the very best hard big wall climbs in the world.

April 2008

Jack Geldard on an early attempt at the new route *Yellow Fever* (7c / E7, 220 metres) on Lemur Wall, Tsaranoro Massif, Madagascar. This was the original first pitch we bolted, and at around 8b+ a successful ascent eluded us in the hot, humid conditions. My solution was to climb a huge hanging vine to the right and then make a cunning traverse (7b) out to the base of the crux third pitch, a bold 7c / E7, which Jack led a few days later.

It was soon clear that the Tarzan vine was our key to free climbing the entire route. We made a belay at the tiny ledge, and I set off on the second pitch: a spectacular traverse that swooped out across the wall to regain the yellow streak. It was getting dark by the time we'd completed it, so we abseiled off and returned to base camp by headtorch.

The following day Jack lead off up what would become the hardest section of the whole route, a huge pitch that took the upper part of the yellow streak. Despite the threat of a huge fall from the most difficult section, he got into the zone and free climbed through this crucial impasse. The final pitch was a relative breeze, and we knew the line was ours. The first climbers to pioneer a route are obliged to give it a name for the record; we had to find a title that fitted in with the febrile theme of the wall. The easier companion route to the left was called *Ebola*, after a particularly virulent tropical virus. Because of the compelling streak in the black granite that had originally drawn us to the line, we decided on *Yellow Fever*. We had created the hardest climb on Lemur Wall. The experience of devising this route, my modification to the line to make it possible as a free climb, then Jack's big lead on the crux pitch was certainly one of the more memorable challenges either of us had faced in twenty years of climbing.

Flushed with success from *Yellow Fever*, James McHaffie and I turned our attention to the project known as *Tough Enough* on the West Face of Karimbony, the awe-inspiring granite monolith that dominates the right hand side of the Tsaranoro Massif. This huge, featureless expanse of rock gleams in the morning sun as if someone had cheesewired a thousand foot chunk of marzipan.

On first acquaintance, it is hard to imagine how it would be possible to free climb the west face at all. No consistent line leads up it. Spidery flakes and tiny cracks spiral through the bright green lichen, heading nowhere. There is barely a single ledge anywhere on the wall big enough to balance on without a handhold. Many of the holds are just minute crystals of granite, sometimes only a few millimetres wide. *Tough Enough*, in short, is the definition of futuristic free climbing.

The climb consists of nine separate pitches, and we began our attempts on the lower four pitches of the wall. I made the first free ascent of the introductory pitch quickly, on my first attempt. Later that day, James worked on the very difficult third pitch, whilst I practised the similarly tricky one below it. At nightfall, we abseiled back to the base of the wall, and made the familiar return to base camp through the jungle by headtorch. The following day, James and I succeeded in free climbing the two hard pitches we'd rehearsed the previous afternoon. We were in high spirits, and managed to climb the fourth pitch afterwards, just before it got dark.

After a rest day, we hiked up to the top of Karimbony to approach the upper pitches from above. Abseiling over the edge of the West Face gives a major overdose of exposure: sliding down our ropes from the flat summit plateau, we instantly became a pair of puppets on a piece of string, with over a thousand feet of sheer, blank granite between us and the ground. James managed to free climb the ninth pitch of *Tough Enough* – the most difficult section of the entire route – late that afternoon, after a huge fall ended his first attempt high on the headwall.

With only a few days left of our expedition and the possibility of free climbing the entire face looking unlikely, we decided to enjoy climbing a few of the established routes around the Massif. We both almost fell asleep with exhaustion on the summit that evening: the physical and psychological strain of *Tough Enough* was beginning to take its toll. We coiled our ropes and stuffed our climbing gear into our packs, and stumbled down to the fixed ropes above Lemur Wall in the falling dusk. The isolated lights of base camp floated up through the immense darkness like the cockpit of some orbiting space station. Stopping for a rest on a huge boulder on the way down, we looked back in silence at the shadowy form of Karimbony. At the end of our adventures on one of the world's hardest walls, we felt lucky to have been part of the conception of such a magnificent climb, and one that would remain on the radar of the world's most talented climbers for years to come. For my own part, I had been as captivated by the extraordinary landscape of this unique island as much as by the exceptional climbing in the Tsaranoro Massif.

As our departure date grew closer, I had already begun to plan my return to the magic mountains of Madagascar.

A few weeks after our expedition left Madagascar in May 2008, big-wall legend Arnaud Petit arrived in Tsaranoro with a team of top French free climbers. They free climbed several other sections of Tough Enough, *returning to Madagascar again in September to finally free climb all ten pitches of the world's hardest wall. In 2010, 18 year old Czech climbing prodigy Adam Ondra travelled to Madagascar on his school holiday, and made an astonishing one-day free ascent of* Tough Enough, *taking just two falls on the entire route and climbing all the pitches free. The route is one of the most spectacular and sought-after hard big wall climbs in the world.*

Above: Jack Geldard (leading) and James McHaffie (belaying) on the stunning arête of *Rain Boto* (7b+ / E6, 450 metres) on Karimbony, Tsaranoro Massif, Madagascar. **Right:** The Tsaranoro Massif in morning light.

April 2008

Facing East

The Minsk Diaries

You go because you're young and crave excitement, the crunch of your boots in the dust.
You go because you're old and need to understand something before it's too late.
You go to see what will happen.

– Colin Thubron

It was late afternoon when the plane hit the runway at Noi Bai airport, and my blood was running hard. The first time you arrive, southeast Asia hits you like the gust of an incoming typhoon. The yellow sky has a sudden magnitude. The evening air smells of dust and smoke and drains. And people do almost everything differently here.

I'd ridden dirt bikes as a teenager, but I learnt to ride a motorcycle for real in the morning rush hour on the outskirts of Hanoi's French Quarter. My two options of sink or swim couldn't have been clearer.

'You must look both ways, every time you go', Mr Cuong had told me in the refuge of his tiny workshop off Rue N'Oc Quen. I'd found out about Mr Cuong, the capital's celebrated dealer of Minsk motorcycles, via an intricate series of tip-offs from Mr Hoi at the Bau Long Hotel. The Bau Long is a glorious old place in the heart of the French Quarter, and it would become my second home between two journeys through the northern mountains.

After a long conversation charting the entire Hoi family tree, Mr Hoi's brother-in-law finally gave me a lift to Mr Cuong's workshop on the back of a scooter. We wound through the tiny lanes closely packed with artisans' stores and overhung by balconies of cascading creepers before making a sharp turn down a slightly wider alley. The heady, slightly sweet smell of petrol fumes mixed with two-stroke oil wafted from the open workshop. Motorcycle components were scattered like spilt beans on the street outside. Mr Cuong greeted us with a big smile that spread across his lean, intelligent face.

'Ah, Mr David, we have been expecting you. We are preparing strong Russian motorcycle for you!'

'That's great, Mr Cuong, thankyou. Do you think I'll be able to take it later today?'

'Yes, today certainly. Or maybe tomorrow. Before that you can be visiting our city.'

'Okay, great… so I could collect the bike tomorrow then?'

'Certainly, very soon, maybe tomorrow. Or Wednesday, early morning. We call you.'

Cuong's 'very soon' captured the unique entity sometimes referred to as 'Asian time'. His business was not organised around deadlines and targets. Work was simply done. It could be today, or tomorrow, or the next day. The elegant logic of this system is infuriating to many

Westerners, but the enforced delay allowed me to explore Vietnam's enchanting capital at leisure.

Later that evening, I walked back to the Bau Long along the northern edge of Hoan Kiem. The city lights reflected off the dark water in a mixture of smudged neon and black ink. The narrow reception appeared to be deserted until I picked up the metronomic tones of Mr Hoi's ancient grandmother snoring quietly behind the desk. At the same time, I spotted a note in my name pinned to the board above the desk: *Minsk ready. See you morning time. Mr Cuong.*

I crept upstairs to my room on the roof and walked out on the balcony. The night air had a welcome chill after the humidity of the day, a reminder of the imminent approach of winter. I inhaled it deeply, contemplating the unknown roads of my adventure that lay ahead. The lights of Hanoi's French Quarter flickered like magic lanterns in the growing dark. I'd arrived at the beginning of my journey.

I rode north out of the city in the coolness of dawn, passing the shadow-boxers on the edge of Hoan Kiem Lake and women with coloured garlands making their way to the early morning flower market. It was more than five years since I'd ridden a motorbike, and the unique Vietnamese system of traffic flow was something of a baptism of fire. Weaving through the multi-directional chaos of the main intersection before the bridge over the Red River, my new found confidence on two wheels was chastised as I watched a blind man make his way with a slow assuredness across at least seven lanes of traffic. It is said of Vietnam that every time you walk into the street, you'll meet a hero. It didn't take me long to find out that heroes come in a thousand disguises in this country, and that none of them wear medals.

After leaving Hoa Bin and the coastal plain, the legendary Highway 6 winds its way northwest from Hanoi into the mountains of Lai Chau province, the most northwesterly part of the country, which borders Laos to the west and China to the north. The potholed tarmac turned to dirt as the road wound into the hills above Hoa Bin. At a narrow col before a steep descent I stopped close to some roadworkers, who immediately invited me over to drink tea under their tarpaulin. The Vietnamese taste for green tea so strong and thick you can stand an upright chopstick in it is wasted on me, but I shared some nonetheless, glad of their hospitality. Afterwards, they passed me

their huge tobacco pipe. I took a drag and spluttered, unused to the acrid smoke and fierce nicotine hit. This produced convulsions of laughter among my companions, and bright smiles flashed through the smoky air.

That night I slept in the makeshift bamboo shack of another group of roadworkers. They had been toiling all day to clear a landslide, a common problem on the roads of northern Vietnam. It was late by the time they'd blasted the last of the rubble away, and they were adamant that I should stay with them instead of continuing on in the dark to Thao Nguyen, fifty kilometres to the north. We stayed up late that night, drinking their home-brewed sake and playing cards. When I said goodbye and made ready to leave early the next day, the wife of one of the workmen, Mai, refused to let me go without a bowl of hot noodle soup. I was hungry, and it was one of the best breakfasts I've ever had. Mai's simple, sacred gesture in the cool dawn air would stay with me more vividly than any good luck charm for the next six months.

I arrived in S'on La at sundown, covered in the thick red dust characteristic of Vietnam's northern roads. It had been an exhilarating day. The air was cold as the wind came down off the mountains and contoured through the deep limestone valley. Some of the women here wore the brightly coloured headscarves of the White Thai, their teeth jet black from years of chewing beetle nut. As I travelled north, the Honda scooters of Hanoi and the lowlands were quickly losing favour to the more robust, archaic Minsk. I was now in familiar company on these mountain roads.

The next day I had a flat tyre on the long descent into the valley north of the small town of Tuan Giao. Just west of here lies the old garrison of Dien Bien Phu where the Viet Minh forces finally ended the French occupation of what they called Indo-China in 1954. I've changed many bike tyres over the years, but find it hard to recall a more laid-back place to have a puncture than on that long hill into the Luan Chao valley. High overhead, two eagles circled on a thermal. The green thread of the valley twisted north like a piece of twine spun between the mountains. I had only been there for a few minutes, finding the necessary tools and the spare tube, when a local man stopped to see what I was doing. It quickly became obvious he was an expert Minsk mechanic, and gave me an impromptu lesson on the rear drive train and brake assembly of this vintage Russian machine in beautifully concise broken English.

'See, this one go this way' he said as he dismantled the hub.

'Two bolt. Like this. Then sprocket, quick fix. No problem.'

'Thanks very much' I replied, enthusiastically testing about half of my entire Vietnamese vocabulary in one sentence. My companion burst into friendly laughter. Vietnamese is a complex, tonal language, and later that evening I worked out that I'd probably told him 'my enormous duck is grateful'.

This episode, like my impromptu evening with the roadworkers above Mai Chau, left me with an overpowering sense of the communal spirit of the north Vietnamese. It is underscored by an intensely energetic practicality, and an unselfish willingness to help others. Both the French and (later and more disastrously) the Americans gravely underestimated the power of this communality in the form of the north Vietnamese fighting spirit.

What the Viet Minh forces accomplished at Dien Bien Phu in 1954 should have made U.S. President Lyndon Johnson think twice when he said, on 24th November 1963 'the battle against communism… must be joined… with strength and determination'.

Johnson was instrumental in escalating the Vietnam War, the most deadly conflict of the late twentieth century which killed somewhere between 3 and 4 million Vietnamese, 1.5 to 2 million Cambodian and Laotians, and circa 60,000 American soldiers. Johnson might have thought twice, perhaps, about his hawkish response to the Viet Cong in the mid 1960s had he known his history. He should have remembered how the Viet Minh foot soldiers encircled and then cut off the massively better armed and equipped French garrison at Dien Bien Phu under the command of the extraordinary General Võ Nguyên Giáp. He should have remembered the terrified disbelief of the French when the Viet Minh commenced artillery fire from the mountains high above the town: Giáp's soldiers had hauled their antique weaponry up the mountains around the garrison by hand using ropes, mainly under cover of night, rendering the French garrison a gigantic sitting duck.

I'd lost an hour fixing the puncture, and it was already late in the day. Beyond Ban Nam Nen, the broken asphalt turned back to dirt, and I rode on hard towards the head of the valley. The Minsk's dustcloud sank fast in the cooling evening air. When biking in hot weather at this time of day, swarms of insects suddenly fill the air and glasses or a visor are essential to keep them from your eyes. I had to stop several times to clear my lenses of squashed flies. Each time, I was glad of the chance to take in the red and green mountains that had begun to rise high on both sides of the valley. I stopped for a final time on the col before the endless switchbacks down to Lai Cao, as the evening mist began to thicken on the rice fields a thousand metres below.

A few days later, I attempted to cross a high pass in the province of Th'a Nugen and over to the valley of the Song Da, the Black River. The speculative route I took was defined by the key on my large scale Nelles map as an 'unclassified road/cart track'. I had travelled down such roads before, and expected the Minsk would take such a route in its stride. As I gained height in the lengthening shadows of evening, the road deteriorated into single track too narrow for a horse, let alone a vehicle, and I began to distrust both my judgement and the cartography of my 1:1,500,000 scale map. At dusk, I arrived in the remote village of Th'on Ban Doc, its bamboo houses clinging on stilts to the mountainside which neither roads nor electricity had yet reached. In 2003, this region was still populated almost exclusively by the White Thai people, one of the numerous indigenous tribes of northern Vietnam that the Vietnamese government euphemistically calls 'the ethnic minorities of Vietnam', ignoring the fact that outside the larger towns relatively few ethnic Vietnamese live in these remote northern hills.

Before long I was surrounded by several dozen children, all of whom watched me intently, silently fascinated by my northern European features and blond hair. I was invited to stay in the village that night by the couple who ran the village school, who were of Vietnamese ethnicity and, amazingly, spoke some English. They told me that only a few old people

in Th'on Ban Doc had seen a white person before, and that none had ever visited the village. I must have seemed a strange, unexpected guest that night in this remote river valley high in the mountains of Vietnam.

Saying goodbye to my hosts the next morning, I felt fortunate to have been their first foreign visitor, and curious as to what might have changed in Th'on Ban Doc were I to return ten or twenty years from now. Would a metalled road have replaced that precarious trail, clinging to the mountain slopes by the narrowest of margins? The subsistence-based agricultural system and traditional way of life here is made possible, at least in part, by its relative inaccessibility, which is a natural barrier to both tourism and outward migration.

I turned the Minsk to the south and out of sight of the Da valley as smoke rose from brushwood fires on the edge of the steep terraced fields where buffalo and horses grazed; a sight familiar to anyone who has travelled in the high country of northern Vietnam.

The ride back to Hanoi that day was long but incredibly exhilarating, and remains of the best days of motorcycling I can remember. I left Thon Ban Doc at six-thirty that morning, and arrived back in the Bau Long Hotel just after ten in the evening. At Bao Ha, I took the dirt road that follows the west bank of the Red River downstream to Van Yen, where a tiny ferry – just large enough to squeeze a small motorcycle on – allows a better road on the east bank to be picked up. I followed it to the larger town of Yen Bai, from where a glorious ride up into the hills took me over to Don Hung and Highway 2. The final few hours of the day, battling across Viet Tri and then on down the Noi Bai freeway (Vietnam's only dual-carriageway in 2003, and one of the country's busiest roads) in the dark was particularly hard going. I shadowed the slipstreams of the bigger truck for protection from other, mainly unlit vehicles. I'd ride like this until the dust got too much to bear, and I'd seek respite in the slow lane. But finding my way back into central Hanoi was easier than expected. City lights and well-lit roads are a blessing after night riding. I crashed out almost instantly after inhaling a bowl of noodle soup and slept solidly for eleven hours.

Left to right: Underneath Vietnam's highest peak, Fanispan, as evening gathers towards the end of the first week on the road. | The remote mountain village of Th'on Ban Doc in Vietnam's northern highlands where I had an unplanned overnight stop after making various map-reading errors. | Boats on the Song Hong (Red River) just outside Hanoi at sundown. | Many northern Vietnamese still wear their iconic traditional wide-brimmed hats when working in the fields. These two farmers are carrying sugar cane using shoulder-trestles down a road outside Yen Bai, a provincial town three hours north of Hanoi.

November 2003

I woke to the mingled sounds of motorcycle horns and exhausts, and the clanging of the gigantic metal spatulas the noodle-stall women use to turn the contents of their woks, and the rattle of vegetable-carts rolling on the cobbles. My body was deliciously tired from yesterday's fourteen-hour ride, but I felt a sharp clarity of thought distilled by my first journey into the mountains of east Asia.

I left Hanoi for the final time the following afternoon, on the notorious Highway 1 that joins the capital with Ho Chi Minh City (formerly Saigon) in the south. This route is also known as 'The Highway of Death' on account of the disproportionate number of fatalities it sees – hardly surprising considering the volume, speed and anarchy of its traffic. All vehicles, from buffalo-carts to trucks, few of which are likely to possess either lights or brakes, must use and compete for the same unmarked, undivided strip of tarmac. When running this gauntlet on a motorcycle, you can quickly sympathise with the great traveller Wilfred Thesiger's sentiment that 'the most destructive invention of the twentieth century [was] the internal combustion engine'. The combined effect of high speed chaos is amplified by the presence of Vietnam's main north-south rail line, which in some places runs very close to the road. The madness of this motorised version of Russian Roulette was grimly illustrated by the hapless scooter rider who recklessly swerved off the road just to my left and was promptly crushed by a passing train. I didn't actually witness his death, but heard the sickening crunch of metal, flesh and bone over the devilish din of the road.

I stopped a short distance ahead, for a much-needed drink of water to quell the rising surge of nausea in my stomach. In response to what was evidently a regular event, a woman tending the noodle stall opposite quickly scurried across the road with a white sheet, in which she wrapped the man's headless, bloodstained corpse. She neatly, calmly and quickly sealed each end with strong tape, as if she were sealing a parcel: it looked like a procedure she was extremely familiar with. She then scurried back across the road at the first opportunity, to attend to her unwatched wok.

Very slowly and very, very carefully, I steered the Minsk back into the multidirectional chaos of Highway 1. At Hanam, I saw a dusty sign to Chi Ne, a village on the much smaller road to the west. I swung out of the homicidal traffic of the Highway of Death with deep gratitude, as the motorised vision of hell I had just seen faded. As I headed out of Hanam on an empty, levelled dirt road heading west, I could smell the damp freshness of the air coming down off the green hills in the distance, and took a deep breath. Keen to make good progress south, I rode on late into the evening that day, through glorious open country criss-crossed by rice fields that were interrupted occasionally by towers of limestone rising erratically from the plains.

The next day I made much better progress south, enjoying the peace and freedom of open, dusty roads after the mayhem of Highway 1. I arrived at Du Lu'ong, a small garrison town on the Ca river, just after sunset. Tomorrow I would head west over the Cau Treo pass into Laos. That night, over a glass of local sake, I reflected on the miles I'd travelled through the wild northern hills of Vietnam over the past month. A kaleidoscope flashed and turned across the garish walls of the cheap diner where I'd ordered a noodle soup and salad. I felt completely at ease on the road, with the world, and in my own company. And I felt an inexplicable affinity with the rugged hills, red rivers and tough, close-packed villages of northern Vietnam. That night I dreamt of a bright country of green mountains and red deltas, and of a quick-witted, undefeatable people.

I left Vietnam the following morning at the Cau Treo pass. Riding across the long, deserted bridge over the Ca river at dawn, a dusty sun rose over the wide plain to the east. To the south lay Vinh, the sprawling new city built from the rubble of fighting between the French and the Viet Minh in the 1950's and American bombing in the early 70's. The badly potholed road twists out of Du'c Tho and makes a dramatic swing west, disappearing headlong into the dense jungle of the Annam Highlands. I reached the summit of Cau Treo just before

eleven. The misty sky above the jungle changed colour ceaselessly. Blue-grey cloud thickened to black, then cleared. The thick-tangled trees vanished again under curtains of veiled mist. Across the border, Vietnam faded to the east.

After Cau Treo, the road plunges through a steep-sided ravine. Soon the densely wooded hills of Annam break and the land stretches out across a wide flood plain. At the new bridge where the rivers Nhuong and Kading meet, I stopped for a while. The merging waters swirl fiercely here, and with unexpected turbulence from their combined strength. Alone on the empty plain, in the middle on that bridge in the heat of the day, I leaned heavily on the Minsk and felt the vibration of the moving water judder through the bike's heavy frame. The hum of that mountain water through the old machine seemed to anticipate the road ahead, like thunder before rain. I took a last, long look down into the swirling current, then a deep swig of cold water from my flask, and kicked the Minsk into reluctant life. I rode on west into a dazzling blue afternoon, towards Mueng Pakxan, the Mekong river, and another country.

Laos's long, lonely Highway 13 is the only road connecting Pakse and the south of the country with its capital, Vientiane, and the mountainous north. It shadows the Mekong's east bank, following the great river north for almost a thousand kilometres, from the remote frontier-post of Veun Kham on the Cambodian border. From Vientiane, it twists into the mountains of the Xiangkhoang Plateau, eventually descending back to the Mekong at Luang Prabang.

Vientiane in late autumn might be the closest thing to a perfect capital city you can find in the early twenty-first century. A French traveller in the 1950's called it 'Asia's Timbuktu', and with good reason. The city is now more commonly known by its local name, Viangchan, but I prefer the exotic, sultry beauty of the French version. The traffic here is slow and lazy, reflecting the pace of life. The interminable bustle and noise of most Asian cities is conspicuous only by its absence; there is no real rush-hour in Vientiane.

The presence of the Mekong immediately to the south gives the place an implacable timelessness. On the southern fringe of the central quarter the sidewalk merges imperceptibly with the huge sandbanks of the great river. In the strong midday sun, the heat swirls above it and the river floats on curtains of shimmering air. With the coming evening, the reedy, languid smell of the river suffuses the air. In the frequent lulls between passing cars and rickshaws, you can hear the brown water turning and gliding between the sandbars. The current is still strong here, even though the river is almost half a mile wide. It is easy to forget you're more than a thousand miles from where the Mekong meets the South China Sea.

I stayed in Vientiane for a week, and the city was a perfect opportunity to get my bike in the best possible mechanical shape for the road ahead. One morning, on the way to the Chinese embassy to collect a visa, the Minsk suffered the first and most serious of various mechanical failures that would befall it over our six-month journey. Braking for a junction, I made a normal gear-change down into second, and a sudden, monstrous crack erupted from the engine, soon followed by the crunch of shattering shrapnel inside the bike's single cylinder.

If you've ever accidentally left your keys in a trouser pocket and later hear them inside your washing machine on full spin, you'll appreciate the alarming nature of a similar sound coming from the guts of a motorcycle engine. After a few seconds, inevitably, the engine died.

I tried the kick-starter, which was completely stuck, confirming my worst fears. One of the piston rings must have sheared off, hence the shrapnel sound, and a piece of it had jammed between the piston and the cylinder sleeve. The only solution to this was to find someone who could re-bore the cylinder and replace the piston: I thanked my lucky stars it had happened in the capital. The time it took to find a mechanic competent enough to carry out the repair and get the Minsk on the road again gave me the chance to have some much needed down-time from the intensity of my solitary journey.

I left Vientiane later than I planned, partly because of the need to get the bike in good shape, and partly because of a girl from California. Since the bike would undoubtedly have got jealous if I stayed on – and perhaps do something worse to me than destroy its own piston – and because her way was south and mine was north, I rode out of the city on December 10th as the afternoon heat shimmered on the plain to the west. As the shadows lengthened and the air cooled, the southern edge of the Xiangkhoang Plateau buckled the horizon. To the north, a wall of green mountains flashed in the day's last light. A shiver of excitement went down my spine: I would ride that way tomorrow. I aimed to stop at Vang Vieng for the night before making a dawn start for Luang Prabang.

Rising at dawn and leaving very early was a habit I'd got into in Vietnam. When you're travelling on a bike, it's wise to make good use of all the hours of light available. Riding in the dark is better as a last resort than a regular habit. Some of the best things about adventure motorcycling in Asia are the things that happen in the early morning: feeling the cool rush of the morning air as you shift into gear and hit the road, the smell of the new day breaking across the hills, greeting farmers on their way to work, and hearing the bright, bubbling chatter of local kids walking to school with dusty shoes.

Almost as soon as I left Vang Vieng on Highway 13, the country changed immediately. From the long plains of the Mekong the land rises in sweeps of hills scored with terraced fields. Quickly, without warning, the terraces are engulfed by jungle mountains too steep for cultivation. Thin wands of mist began to streak the highest trees, refracting the sun into columns of green and white light. On the first big climb of the day out of Ban Phatang, the Minsk's rebuilt cylinder hummed with new confidence.

I began the ascent of Highway 13's highest pass in the late afternoon. Leaving Muang Kasi, a windswept one-horse village with a wild-west air, I felt the unmistakable chill of winter for the first time. A cold wind blew down the valley, and odd, stray gusts kicked up dust devils in the dirt. I turned up the collar on my jacket to reduce the chill. Shivering, I thought about Natalie heading south into new countries and different climates. Knowing I'd probably never see her again, I felt glad our journeys had crossed, like two dragonflies brushing wings in the dark.

I saw the stray flare of metallic red of a car bonnet amid the ochre leaves and road dust as I passed, almost as an afterthought. Stopping a short distance further on, I walked back to discover the identity of that alien colour in this rugged land. Weeds grew through the buckled wheels and empty windscreen, giant bamboo sprouted from the rust of the big V8 and the paint flaked off like ash under my fingers. It was an early 70's Pontiac Firebird, one of the most desirable American sports cars of its era. It looked like it hadn't moved an inch for twenty five years. What strange events had left it to rust here, on the summit of one of the highest passes on the Xiangkhoang Plateau? Had some flashy U.S. Army Captain been forced to abandon it here in the chaos of the American withdrawal from Vietnam?

Two boys suddenly poked their heads above the driver's side wing, laughing innocently. I couldn't help but do the same. Our laughter broke my reflective mood, and I showed the inquisitive boys my map. In the most rural areas of south east Asia, few people have seen detailed maps of any kind of their home region. These two were particularly captivated by the sight of their village and the mountains around it in two dimensions, creased and held together with sellotape.

'Look, the Mekong' I said, pointing to the blue line of the great river cutting through the darker swathes of the mountains.

'Ah, Meaak-Hong' they said, pronouncing the great river's name as they pointed west towards it with the heavy local emphasis on the second syllable. Their dark eyes lit up as they recognised the river on the map, as if they somehow understood its enormous power.

I stopped for a final time that day on the last high pass of Highway 13, before the road twists down the long hill to Xiang Ngeun and the final stretch back to the Mekong and Luang Prabang. There were blue-grey clouds shrouding the higher mountains to the north. A cold wind blew across the shoulder of the ridge and through the narrow gap in the trees at the summit of the pass. A wave of lonely delight swept over me as I sheltered behind the bike, drinking green tea from my flask, watching the world turn as the light drained out. I stayed there for a while, watching the sky steadily darken in the east. When the air grew colder, I started the bike and rode on into the evening. I could see the lights of distant trucks winding up the hill far below, and flicked the switch on my own headlight as I began the descent.

After travelling four thousand miles through Yunnan and Sichaun in southern China, at the beginning of January I crossed the Mekong from Ban Huai Sai in Laos to Chiang Khong in Thailand. I'd been on the road just two months but it already felt like years. From here, my plan was as ambitious as it was loose. I aimed to ride through the mountainous north of the country before heading south and east, across the plains of Phitsanulok and Chaiyaphum, and crossing into the remote jungle of northern Cambodia just south of Surin. Then I'd head west for the Gulf coast and take the road south from Bangkok down the Kra Isthmus. After that, improvisation would be my strongest ally. From the very beginning of this journey, I'd sought to travel by instinct. As I rolled the Minsk off a dugout canoe at Chiang Khong in northwest Thailand, I felt that the roads I'd already travelled had been a strong initiation for what was going to happen next.

The visible difference between the Mekong's east bank at Ban Huai Sai in Laos to the much more modern country I found on the river's other side captured the gigantic cultural and economic contrasts visible everywhere in the developing world. The opposition between the sleepy, dusty, one-street town of Ban Huai Sai and its bustling counterpoint to the west defined the separation of developing Asia from the rapidly Westernising, obsessively modern Asia of Thailand in the early twenty-first century.

Rolling into Thailand felt like entering a new world. Gone were the makeshift roadside bamboo shacks fastened with twine and coconut leaves; gone were the wide-eyed, filthy street kids with tangled black hair that only half concealed their brilliant smiles; gone were the buffalo

meandering unattended through the dust in the evening. The strange sight of more familiar customs replaced them: busy cafés were filled with people working on laptops, reading newspapers, or chatting loudly into mobile phones, and swarms of modern Japanese cars and pickup trucks jostled for position on major intersections.

After stopping briefly in Chiang Khong to change money on the black market (where you always get a better rate), and picking up a few long-overdue spare parts for the Minsk – a new back tyre, spokes, a chainwheel, clutch plates, and a chain – I set off quickly for Mae Chan and Mae Ai, a small hill-town built on a narrow ridge about a hundred kilometres west of the Mekong and just south of the Burmese border. Just north west of here, the Doi Ang Khang poppy fields stretch into the distance towards that elusive country to the north. These fertile plains ringed by green mountains – the heart of the so-called 'Golden Triangle' of global opium production – were one of the major sources of the notoriously pure heroin that circulated among American GIs in the latter years of the Vietnam war.

I stayed that night in Mae Ai in a tiny room that overhung the steep slope of the mountains falling away to the north. I rose in the half-gloom at five thirty, and left as the dawn was just starting to break across the hills to the east. There were blue and red clouds along the horizon, and as the sun rose on the hill down towards Chiang Dao the entire sky reflected the rising sunlight for a few seconds. It was a moment so intensely luminous and so completely three-dimensional that no photograph could ever have reproduced it, and set the tone for a thrilling day's riding.

With its re-bored cylinder and new piston now bedded in, the Minsk was on the best form of the entire trip. The higher quality of the gasoline in Thailand may have helped too, since much of the fuel I'd been running on until now had been of an ambiguous octane rating. In much of developing Asia, petrol is diluted with kerosene, paraffin, alcohol, or any other flammable liquid you can think of. After leaving Pai on the Nam Mae Pai river, I took Highway 1095 around Thailand's extreme northwest tip to Mae Hong Song. It is one of southeast Asia's more spectacular roads, and a motorcyclist's dream: it curls along the Burmese border like a shadow-boxer, shrugging off even the steepest climbs with deep switchbacks, and diving into secret, sharp-edged ravines at a moment's notice. I reached Mae Hong Song, a bustling market town in the country's extreme northwesterly corner, just as the air was cooling and the dusk sky begun to drain

the colour from the hills. Green turned to deep blue and gradually faded to grey, with the shadows of the spines of more distant ridges interlocking and vanishing in the darkness beyond.

Before arriving on the outskirts of Mae Sariang itself, the road climbs over a little pass just north of Pang Mu and plunges into a deep valley. The road here is overhung with black crags that seem to float above the highest trees. Half-lost in the thick, misty air of that jungle evening, I felt that this valley might go on into interminable distance, towards some place lost in time beyond the edge of the map and just out of reach.

I found a simple room in a quiet guesthouse on the edge of the river, and remember it as one of the most beautiful I've ever slept in. There was a bamboo mat on the wooden floor with a candle beside it, a mosquito net, and a table and chair against the wood-panelled wall. That was all. The window was open, and the room smelt of the river outside and the hills beyond it. I sat on the edge of the flat concrete roof and smoked a cigarette as the creatures of the night began their soporific drone.

In this part of Asia, the frogs and cicadas seem to increase their volume as the last strands of light drain out of the sky and the neon bulbs of street vendors begin to flicker. A bright star rose in the southwest and I ate fresh fish from the river for dinner that a little boy brought over in a box on the back of his bicycle. Served with the staple Thai side-dish of rice and vegetables, it was the most delicious thing I'd eaten for months. George Mackay Brown sprung to mind: 'a river fish has been left at my door. / Gifts come like autumn leafage in my doorway.'

The next morning I rose at dawn and left Mae Sariang with unexpected regret: it is the kind of place where time could melt like ice in the sun, where mornings merge with evenings and evenings with night. Perhaps I should have stayed, but I had really got to get going if I was to make it to Prah Nang Bay in the far southwest of the country by the end of January using my chosen route through Cambodia: I had some serious distance to cover.

It was another exhilarating day. After plunging down a series of steep hairpins thirty kilometres south of Mae Sariang, Highway 105 picks up the east bank of the powerful Mae Nam Moei river which rises in the distant highlands of Myanmar. The road shadows the riverbank for over a hundred kilometres, until it reaches the remote border-town of Mae Sot. Eager to make swift progress east, I took a short-cut route over the mountains above the temple of Wat Don Kaeo. The landscape changes as you travel south from the jungle mountains of Chiang Mai

and Mae Hong Song towards Sukhothai and the great central plains of Phitsanulok and Chaiyaphum. The intense green of the steep-sided hills is split by the blue and white flashes of rivers. Eventually, these rivers fade into the ochre vastness of the open land that stretches across the heart of the country. In midwinter, the plains lie parched by months without rain, and the grass turns the same colour as the earth itself.

Thailand's Highway One is the main arterial trunk road connecting Bangkok with the country's second city, Chiang Mai. As I crossed the huge intersection at Tak from west to east, the inexplicable feeling of entering a wilder country washed through me. Perhaps it was the way the sky opened out like a fan in the absence of interruptions like towns and other roads, expanding the horizon in every direction. Or perhaps it was the arrow-straight strip of tarmac that vanished into the haze in the distance ahead. Most of all, perhaps, it was the feeling that very soon I would be crossing the border into Cambodia.

I made it to the small plains city of Phitansulok by dusk that day, riding under the familiar leer of the neon signs scrawled with tightly-packed Thai characters and the occasional bit of pidgin-English. I noticed a sign for 'Chow Mien – Fried Children' scribbled on a blackboard under a noodle stall: a classic among the perpetual comedy of lost translations played out in East Asia.

That night I stayed in a cheap, old-fashioned hotel on the eastern edge of the city, which I chose because it seemed well-placed for my early departure tomorrow on Highway 12, heading east. It was hot that night and I slept directly underneath the old fan, clunking around slowly like a decrepit windmill. The sweet smell of garlic, ginger, and chilli in smoking wok oil still hung in the air; an unmistakable scent of the provincial towns of Thailand, Cambodia, and Malaysia.

When I left Phitansulok at five thirty the next morning, the air was still dark and cool. The road outside was quiet, but the low drone of a heavy truck pulling away from the intersection around the block reminded me that I was on Thailand's arterial east-west highway. For the first time since the jungle mountains of northern Laos, I had to fasten my leather jacket right to the top to keep out the chill. As I swung out of the hotel courtyard and into the street, my headlight beam glanced off a puddle, like the beam of a lighthouse. I had a long journey ahead today.

Given the Minsk's top speed of eighty kilometres per hour, I covered the seven hundred kilometres from Phitansoluk and Buriyam in a respectable twelve hours, with a few stops. In the middle of the vast plains of Nakhon Ratchasima, to the east of Chaiyaphum, the clutch lever warped alarmingly as I changed gear to negotiate some potholes. I then watched in horror as it bent and lazily snapped like a lead pipe. In slow-motion, it fell and vanished into the dust, leaving a useless, sharp stud of cheap Chinese alloy protruding from the lever housing. I thanked my lucky stars that this had happened today in Thailand, where I knew I would find a replacement part, instead of tomorrow in northern Cambodia, where I certainly would not. I put it down to traveller's luck, keeping my fingers crossed that no more serious problems would occur on my journey south for the Gulf.

Sure enough a mechanic's shop appeared on the outskirts of Muang Yang, a tiny place on the Mae Nam Mun river. As I rolled the bike up the ramp I felt like a thirsty traveller who'd just discovered a spring. It only took a few minutes to replace the broken lever with a new Japanese spare, and I bought another before I left just in case. There wouldn't be any well-equipped workshops like this until Phnom Phen, at the very least.

Buriyam is a busy provincial town about sixty kilometres from the Cambodian border, and the sort of place that remains completely off the tourist radar. I wound through the bustling streets as the night-market vendors were opening their stalls, passing a few glum-looking Chinese hotels. The scrum of scooters and bicycles I was in ground to a halt at a crossing. At that moment I noticed a flash of neon from a small café to the right, half-obscured by foliage, with the drawl of Thai pop music trailing out from a ghetto blaster in the yard. It looked like the right kind of place to wind down after my long day of riding across the hot plains. Besides, I was dehydrated and had begun to hallucinate

Left to right: A good road near Cao Bang, northeast Vietnam. | Welding the Minsk's rear dropout after pothole damage in Cambodia. | Early morning light on one of the carved faces of the Bayon, Angkor Thom, Cambodia. | A sign prohibiting fishing with grenades on a dirt road west of Sihanoukville, Cambodia. Due to the quantity of weaponry left in the country, fishing with explosives is a major environmental issue.

November 2003 – January 2004

bottles of cold, sugary liquid touching my lips. I pulled in and cut the engine. My hair was thickly matted with sweat and my skin was covered in a layer of red dust. Dark stains of two-stroke oil ran from the backs of my hands right up my arms. I was completely spent from thirteen hours of riding, and the evening blurred into sleep.

I woke just before dawn on the bamboo floor of the café kitchen to the quiet sounds of the street outside: a lone scooter passing; the distant rumble of a truck; a wok crackling down the alleyway opposite. Toni and Mai, the café's owners and my spontaneous hosts for the night, were still fast asleep on bamboo mats inside. The courtyard was silent in the cool, scented air. I rose quickly and rolled up my sleeping bag, packing my few possessions into the narrow backpack I strapped to the back of the bike. I left a note thanking them for their wonderful hospitality, drank a thick black coffee from a street stall, then rolled the bike down out of the yard. The engine was completely caked in dust from yesterday but started first time. Good on you, Minsk, I thought. I wanted to leave Buriyam as early as possible and make good progress to the border.

An hour before I reached Surin – the last big town before Cambodia and the last place I would find spares for the bike until Siam Riep, over two hundred kilometres to the south – the Minsk threw another of its inexhaustible jokers from the pack of breakdown cards. This time, the rear suspension mount (the piece of metal that attaches the rear shock absorber to the rest of the bike) partially sheared. This was far worse than yesterday's clutch lever problem. It strongly suggested that the bike was in no fit state to take on my intended route, which took in some of southeast Asia's worst roads between the border and the Cambodian capital, Phnom Phen.

This time, yet again, my luck held out against the red jester from Belarus. As always in Thailand, I managed to find a place where I could get the bike back into a functional state. I saw the welding rig out of the corner of my eye, and swung into the yard with an urgency that surprised the two men fixing the dismantled scooter that lay strewn across its concrete floor. They looked up with the uniquely rapid interest of tradesmen who know they've seen something that could quite possibly be a 'big job'.

If Monty Python's Flying Circus had ever been given a brief to design a motorcycle, they would have come up with something very similar, I thought, to this cantankerous contraption that had miraculously got me across seven thousand kilometres of southeast Asia so far. The only added comic feature was my belief in the wretched thing's roadworthiness. An hour later, and with the rear stay now expertly welded back into some sort of shape, I gave the welder a decent tip for his efforts and rolled the Minsk out of the yard with a hasty goodbye. The road from Surin to Kap Choeng, the tiny outpost of Thai civilisation glued to the edge of the Dangrek Mountains, passed without further incident. As I waited in the small queue of jostling locals, mostly Thai traders taking cheap Chinese domestic goods south to the remote jungle villages, I felt a sudden, inexplicable sense of excitement. Perhaps I watched *Apocalypse Now* at an impressionable age, but Cambodia was somewhere I'd always dreamed of arriving. As a teenager, I'd imagined crossing a river overhung with giant trees, where the far bank was a place no modern communications had yet reached. At Kap Choeng, the nearest river is ten kilometres away and most of the tallest trees have been felled, but my sense of childish excitement still remained.

Once I'd got my visa stamped and cleared the border, the country suddenly expanded in front of me. It felt like the curtains of a cinema opening into widescreen. To the south all traces of industrialised, civilised life had vanished, and there was nothing but jungle and swamp stretching beyond the horizon. I couldn't wait to get going. As soon as I'd shaken off the usual coterie of scam-merchants, con-artists, and random space-cadets who predictably appear at border crossings throughout the developing world, I squeezed the Minsk's throttle, stamped into third, and hit the road south. My dustcloud completely obscured the view in the mirror back towards Thailand, and the steady riding of the past ten days quickly disappeared in a thick, red-brown haze. I knew I was in for a tough day.

As I gained speed, the flow of dirt riding quickly returned. My body loosened up with the increasing feedback from the bike as I stood up on the pedals, and I suddenly noticed the machine had begun to shudder alarmingly with the change in angle at every corner. I was concerned about the morning's improvised repair failing, and dropped my speed, taking each bend with more caution than usual. As the ruts deepened, with great relief I realised that the shuddering wasn't a sign of the bike threatening to disintegrate, but of the deepening corrugations on every change in the road's direction.

I made good progress south into the Kampong Highlands, and the road deteriorated with every passing mile. I found myself riding through giant potholes rather than around them; their sheer scale meant that circumnavigation was impossible. It was simply a case of down one side, and up the other. Although the Minsk had begun to produce a new cacophony of shallow, gasping wheezes from the dust-choked carburetor, I felt it was on its best form of the entire journey so far.

It was already late in the afternoon. I knew I had no hope of reaching Siam Riep in daylight, but decided to press on: the thought of finding a clean bed in a quiet room in which to collapse for the night was enough to sustain me through the next six hours of combat motorcycling. As night fell, the jungle grew suddenly, impossibly dark in minutes. I thought of Graham Greene's observation in The Quiet American that 'the men grow old here the same way the sun goes down: they are boys and then they are old men'.

I was enveloped by a wild expanse of darkness stretching infinitely across the land, shrouding everything in its grasp. Just beyond the faint smudge at the edge of the road where dust merged into trees, the brushwood camp fires of local people lit my way far better than my fading headlight beam. The unmistakable smell of chilli and garlic crackling in hot oil – the signature scent of East Asian streets – mingled with the damp cool of the jungle. By the firelight, I could make out the shapes of houses along the roadside. Shadows of villagers hovered between them, sometimes moving imperceptibly, like dreaming ghosts.

This evening, winding slowly south through the western Cambodian jungle by firelight, I felt I'd turned a new corner in my journey. The creature comforts and perfect tarmac of Thailand were gone, replaced by a harsher reality of barely drivable roads and a complete absence of signposts, petrol stations, or anything else a traveller might find useful. All the infrastructure we normally associate with driving simply didn't exist here. If you wanted to get some petrol in the far north of Cambodia in the first years of the twenty-first century, you'd have had to ask someone in a roadside teahouse, who might have a few plastic bottles under their bamboo table.

The last ninety kilometres to Siam Riep took an interminable five hours. My headlight had failed almost completely as the alternator coil was completely clogged with dust, and I rode in the slipstream of a convoy of big trucks on that last stretch, following the movements of their tail lights, trying to anticipate the biggest of the approaching potholes. When the trucks negotiated the largest of all these craters, their lights would disappear almost completely with the sudden change in angle. Facing up as the truck plunged down, they became dim red smudges in the dusty night air. It was the closest thing I've ever experienced to being at sea whilst on land; the complete spatial disorientation of riding without a headlight was amplified by the necessity of using the moving tail-lights as my guide. Occasionally, I'd misjudge a pothole and both the back and front shock absorbers would bottom-out with a sickening crunch. Each time, I thought the Minsk would simply give up the ghost, making a spectacular final protest against its abuse with a gargantuan shearing clunk, as the frame

warped and the crankcase hit the dirt in a hot splash of black oil and shrapnel.

I rode like this for almost four hours. When I thought I couldn't go on much further, I stopped at a roadside tea shack. I was completely exhausted, but at the same time strangely energised. There is a reserve energy tank in a person's body that can only be switched on in certain situations, and only when all available blood-sugar and fluid has been used up. Tonight, somewhere in Cambodia, was one such time.

'Is it far, Siam Riep' I enquired in French to the dreamy girl who'd served me tea, with the hope that she'd understand it.

'No, no, not that far' she replied to my amazement in perfect French.

Her bright, faraway smile and the hot tea she brought gave me a renewed burst of energy, and I set out on the final stretch of my epic day. The convoy of trucks were far ahead by now, rolling east into the night, towards Pnomh Phen and the Mekong Delta.

The air changed as I set out, and a cool dampness blew in off the approaching trees. Western Cambodia was heavily deforested by the Khmer Rouge, but much of the old jungle around the ruins of Angkor – the extraordinarily advanced civilisation that existed here over a millennia ago – remains, thankfully, intact.

I finally arrived in Siam Reap around ten thirty. I felt like I'd been playing a fourteen hour chess match whilst riding a wild horse: I was completely beat. Following my instincts, I found a quiet place to stay on the edge of town. I ate some noodles, struggling with the effort of twirling them around my chopsticks, and drank a beer. When you're really tired from a long journey involving a lot of physical exertion, the feeling of stretching out on freshly washed linen is the most delicious thing in the world. The night was quite cool, so I turned the fan off and listened to the castanet drone of cicadas until I fell into a long, dreamless sleep.

I woke to a shaft of bright sunlight falling through a chink in the shutters. I must have slept in, I thought, reaching for my watch. It showed 7.45: a serious lie-in after a run of pre-dawn starts. In the east, everyone rises with the sun; this morning, waking well after sunrise

felt like utter decadence, which was only enhanced when I realised I didn't have to leave Siam Riep until Thursday. It was only Monday; just the prospect of three whole days without riding distance felt like I'd been given a first class ticket to the most luxurious hotel on the planet. But all I had here was a simple, clean room with a mango tree outside the window. Luxury is a relative concept, after all.

Later that afternoon, reading by the pool of an uptown hotel under the cool shade of a pair of coconut trees, I met Sonya. She taught English and French at a school for Cambodian orphans set up by French missionaries. Born in Marseille, she'd spent most of her life moving. She was forty-one, but looked a decade younger. She had that distinctive beauty unique to French women in early middle-age: her whole being shimmered with a dusky, sophisticated sensuality. She and her ex-husband, who worked for the UN, had moved here from Switzerland for a change of scene. Perhaps the cultural shift had been too much; their marriage had fallen apart, she said. There was a deep, mysterious sadness in her bright green eyes. Sometimes, when I told her of my journey, it faded and was replaced by a deep luminescence, as if she were trying to reach back to a part of her life that was locked away in time and imagination.

When she brushed her oil-dark hair away from her eyes as we were talking, I felt that our conversation had triggered a feeling that she'd lost something precious, something she thought she might never get back.

In the growing dark, we shared a cigarette under the green thickness of the papaya trees in the back garden. The air was very quiet and still, except for the faint drone of cicadas somewhere else, somewhere out there in the jungle. I looked across and saw that she was trying not to breathe, and her eyes were half-closed.

'Shhhhhh', Sonya whispered, so quietly I could barely hear her, as if she were trying not to disturb the sticky, inky silence of the Cambodian night. I felt she wanted us to become part of it, standing there alone, encased in that immense black space stretching into the outer dark of the jungle, into its old stones, its tangled trees, and its forgotten mysteries.

Left to right: The Minsk on the beach at Sihanoukeville, southern Cambodia. | Kids on a raft-ferry on one of the many river crossings on the road between Sihanoukville, Cambodia and Koh Kong, Thailand. | Arriving in Kuala Lumpur, Malaysia. | A rice farmer on a stormy evening in central Sumatra, Indonesia. | A traditional Bartak tomb on Samosir Island, Lake Toba, central Sumatra. | Bartak houses on the east shore of Lake Toba, central Sumatra. | Sunrise at Sorake Bay, Nias Island, Sumatra.

January 2004 – April 2004

The next morning, I left Siam Riep at dawn as a huge, blood-red sun was rising in the southeast sky. The air felt like it was going to get hot out here, on the empty plains of the interior. As I rode east, the heat built up relentlessly, and the road worsened. The good asphalt around Siam Riep was completely gone, replaced with huge, bone-jarring potholes and giant ruts. These craters were the results of zero maintenance for several decades, coupled with the fact that even in the summer rainy season, big trucks still made their way, painfully slowly, across the country, gouging ever deeper corrugations in the mud and dirt. I couldn't begin to imagine how hideous this journey would be during the monsoon.

After a couple of hours, the plain began to wobble under the sun and only the movement of riding would create a tolerable temperature. Having already run out of the insufficient water I'd filled up in Siam Riep, I stopped at a coconut stall somewhere in the middle of Cambodia, in the white heat of the day. Nothing moved. On the road, and on the plain, everything was perfectly still. It felt as if the earth itself was being pressed down by the huge, relentless weight of the heat shimmering above it.

The boy at the coconut stall had a tiny umbrella, which gave him just enough shade to cower under in the presumably long intervals between customers. He cracked open a coconut with a single, expert blow from a machete, inserted an enormous straw, and handed it to me. There is absolutely nothing that tastes better than cold, fresh coconut juice when you're really hot and really thirsty. I drank the whole thing

without stopping. When I'd finished, I asked for another. With a bright smile, the boy grabbed the biggest one in his bamboo basket. I sat under the tiny patch of shade under his umbrella, drinking the second coconut, feeling the life return to my parched body. Dehydration is one of the biggest dangers of adventure motorcycling in hot countries, and today I'd had a full dose of it. Conscious of the inherent dangers of being dehydrated – instant lack of concentration, spatial disorientation, and delayed reaction time – I stopped regularly to drink through the rest of that hot afternoon.

Approaching Pnomh Phen at sunset, the city emerged like a dream-vision from the far bank of the Mekong. You can smell the great river long before you see it; here, still a few hundred kilometres from the sea, it is almost a mile wide. Underneath the new steel, the murky water flows resolutely south towards the South China Sea.

Ramshackle high-rise blocks and old wooden-rafted houses were jumbled together with delightful recklessness. The sudden brightness of washing hanging out to dry transformed the drab squalor into instant, colourful life. In the lull between waves of traffic, the sound of crackling woks spat hot oil into the evening. That unmistakable east Asian smell of ginger, chilli and garlic frying reminded me that I'd not eaten for twelve hours; I needed to find a place to stay and get some dinner.

Arriving in a developing world capital at dusk after riding a motorcycle all day is the least relaxing form of arrival in a new place it is possible to experience, short of actually being thrown in jail. I turned off the main drag and followed signs for a hotel down a lively side-street packed with stalls that sold everything from cheap, corrupted petrol to deep fried insects. I checked in, and took a cold shower. Standing under the delicious, refreshing rush of water, I felt layer after layer of dust and grime rinsing out of my hair and skin. Having a cold shower with soap is one of the best physical experiences you can have when you've been riding a bike for a whole day in tropical conditions; I had to unclog the plug of sand and silt at least three times.

It was completely dark outside by the time I flung open the wooden shutters and looked out into the street. Men were packing up their wares around the daytime stalls and women were bustling around setting up the night market. As in every city across the world, the streets changed with the coming of night. The bright, busy reality of the day was replaced with something quite different; a smokier, stranger, more mysterious energy.

I went out and ordered some 'special noodles' from the woman with the biggest, smokiest, strangest-looking wok along the entire street, based on the principle that you should try everything once. She said something in Khmer to her small assistant who fetched a pot of live, writhing creatures. My empty stomach turned. As she grabbed the pot, something large and hairy fell out. So that was what 'special noodles' meant in this part of Phnom Phen: Tarantula Noodles. Spidery legs had been plucked and battered, and were now bubbling in hot oil. I was starving, and needed to eat something, spider or no spider. The first bite was crunchy, the second was slightly more crunchy, and on the third my teeth sank into a fat, succulent pod, about the size of a matchbox. Amazingly, it was delicious. And it's not every night that you clasp a deep fried tarantula head between your teeth, after all.

A month later, after riding down the Gulf of Thailand and across to the west coast, our twin-engined speedboat gurgled out from the pier into the slow current, then accelerated hard as it cleared the sandbar at the mouth of the river. Limestone towers rose along the horizon. Ko Laoliang, a tiny island in the Surin Archipelago about twenty miles off Thailand's south west coast, was the break from the road I'd been searching for intently, but never quite found. In the few weeks I spent living and climbing there, the dusty hills of East Asia faded into a dream-sequence, locked up with the battered Minsk in the chandler's shed by the pier.

On rest days from climbing we'd head out in longtail boats to catch fish, swim, and play chess until late in the evening. It was easy to imagine staying there indefinitely, casting adrift on the complex currents that twist between the islands. One morning, I peered over the edge of a longtail beyond the point of the reef, where the seabed plunges into darkness. Shadows of sharks spiralled under us in pursuit of tuna, headed for other islands to the south and west. Laoliang was a great recharging place just beyond the mid-point of my journey, and without the respite it offered I would never have made it as far as I did. But I couldn't stay there for too long or else my momentum would be lost, so when my friends left for home I headed south for Malaysia.

For the last six weeks of my journey, a current swept through me stronger than any I'd yet encountered: too strong even to stop and climb. Each day, I'd be on the bike by dawn, and travel by instinct. I rode south for two days straight and arrived in downtown Kuala Lumpur black with oil and dust. But there was no time to lose: with an Indonesian general election less than two months away, and the historical reluctance of their authorities to grant visas at politically sensitive times, I had to cross the Malacca Straits as soon as I could.

Two days later, I rode the Minsk up a plank on the Malacca docks and on to a boat for Sumatra. Night fell as we approached the low-lying, murky, mangrove-enchanted coast. A dim fog of shore fires blew across the dense jungle beyond the black water of the Straits, and the shadows of big trees loomed beyond it. The sea smelt of oil and salt and heat as the lights of fishermen crossed our wake. I'd reached the final stage of my journey.

A brief logistical inconvenience delayed my Indonesian adventure: the Minsk was impounded on arrival in Dumai by Indonesian customs police because I had no Carnet [an internationally recognised vehicle passport]. I was faced with no other option than to steal my own bike back before dawn from their compound. My plan worked: the compound was guarded only by a fat, snoring policeman and an emaciated cat. Flushed with success, I rode into the jungle bound for Pekanbaru at high speed, only to be stopped five hours later by a heavily armed Indonesian military police roadblock. Surrounded by soldiers with assault rifles, and

Left to right: Evening falls after a thunderstorm on the rice fields near Danu Ranau, south Sumatra. | Approaching Wonosobo on central Java's Dieng Plateau and the easternmost point of my journey. | Kids on the beach at Sorake Bay, Pulas Nias, Indonesia. | Danu Ranau, south Sumatra. | Wild flowers grow by the roadside near a Christian church, central Sumatra. | A farmer burns stubble in a field near Wonosobo, central Java. | On the way to Indonesia's bustling capital the morning after my lucky escape with the timber truck. | In Malaysia's southern highlands on the way to Johur Bahru, Singapore, and the end of my journey.

April – May 2004

quickly bundled into a truck heading back for a police cell in Dumai, my only remaining option was to befriend – and then to bribe – the customs officer in charge into making a temporary Carnet for the Minsk. With all the paperwork done, the next morning I hit the road north for the volcanic highlands of central Sumatra.

Most days, I'd ride on into the dark after the evening mist had swirled low over the rice fields. I rode northwards into the province of Aceh, then troubled by a long-running civil war. A week later, I waited on the quay at Silbolga for the night boat to Pulau Nias. The old ferry rumbled slowly out into the tide as lightning hit Musala Island to the south. It was still dark when I rolled off the boat at Gunungsitoli, with the air full of thunder and mosquitoes. But the storm passed, and in the afternoon I made good time down the east coast to Sorake Bay. I stayed there for a couple of days – my only respite from the road in an entire month of continuous travelling in Sumatra and Java – in a small wooden shack on stilts by the low stone breakwater under the first line of coconut trees. The first morning, I woke to an oily sun recoiling off the triple-overhead surf that broke hard on the outer reef. By evening, the sound of the sea was as loud as a low-flying plane as the wind picked up. The village kids raced around with sticks, whistling and laughing, trying to capture fugitive coconuts. I could have stayed for weeks, but my visa only lasted one month. I had to get back on the road if I was to complete what I had in mind. In ten days of hard riding south and east, I made it as far as Wonosoba,

a beautiful highland town on the edge of the Dieng Plateau in central Java. Once there, I had to acknowledge that I'd come far enough, and there was no way I'd get back to Dumai before my visa ran out if I carried on east.

Midnight. The road trembled like the surface of a beaten drum. Big trucks bear down on my battered Minsk, their headlights blown out, headed east for Surabaya, Yogyakarta, or god knows where. An hour from the eastern suburbs of Jakarta, I'm eighteen hours deep on my longest day of riding on the entire trip. In mountaineering, the most dangerous part of a climb is the descent. Likewise, the most dangerous part of adventure motorcycling is the last few hours of a very long day. I was dehydrated, hypoglycemic, and badly needed to find a place to sleep. I saw a hotel sign flickering amid a cluster of shabby neon and broken glass on the road's far side, checked my mirrors, and turned right.

In a split-second, the air-blast hit me from behind as it passed, and a smoke-machine of oil and diesel fumes knocked me sideways. The huge, unlit timber truck howled its horn like a deathknell and snarled off into the thick Indonesian night, a black rider on the dark.

Shaken, I pulled into the sanctuary of a concrete yard stalked by scowling dogs and hunkering shadows. I hit the kill switch to cut the engine and noticed that my left mirror wasn't there: the truck had clipped it off as it passed. As near-misses go, as Captain Willard says of Colonel Kurtz: 'He was close. He was real close'. I parked up, checked into a filthy one-dollar room, smoked a Gudang Garam, took a cold shower, and slept the sleep of the dead till dawn.

In Francis Ford Coppola's masterpiece *Apocalypse Now* the only two survivors from the mission to kill Colonel Kurtz are the battle-hardened, pragmatic Captain Willard and the soul-searching, starry-eyed Californian surfer, Lance Johnson.

Willard makes it by thinking he knows what he's doing and improvising when he needs to. Lance Johnson makes it by understanding he doesn't know what he's doing, and believing in what he improvises.

My journey, I guess, was more like Lance's than the Captain's.

Rising the next morning feeling as lucky to be alive as I'd ever been, I hit the road west for Indonesia's sprawling capital city, Jakarta. Beyond it lay the ferry back to Sumatra, a hot ride through the eastern jungle to Pekanbaru and on to Dumai and the boat back across the Malacca Straits, where I'd head south to reach the Minsk's final resting place in an Indian motorcycle collector's garage in Johur Bahru, Malaysia.

That the bike made it to the end of our journey is a testament to the simplicity of Soviet engineering, to the rambunctious mechanics of southeast Asia, and the value of a touch of Anglo-Saxon tenacity.

That I made it to the end, on the other hand, is proof of remembering good luck isn't something you wait for, but something you make.

*'Facing East' is a compilation of a series of extracts from my journal from an unsupported, solo motorcycle expedition in East Asia I made between November 2003 and May 2004. I travelled circa 15,000 kilometres through eight countries, beginning in Hanoi, Vietnam and ending in Singapore. The motorcycle I used for the entire trip (outside China) was the two-stroke 125cc 'Minsk', a Soviet-era two-stroke machine made in Belarus and still widely used in northern Vietnam. It survived to the finish line, although the steel frame had been welded in **seventeen** separate places by the end of the expedition. I also got through twelve tyres, three chains, two rear sprockets, two chainwheels, four air filters, fourteen fuel filters, two electrical coils, eight sets of front suspension seals, three sets of rear shocks, six sets of brake shoes, five sets of clutch plates, and an unknown quantity of two-stroke oil. I purchased the Minsk from Cuong's Motorcycle Adventures in Rue N'oc Quen, Hanoi, Vietnam for $350 and sold it Johur Bahru, Malaysia at the end of the expedition for $50 to a local motorcycle collector of South Indian origin. The Minsk is still a popular model of motorcycle in Vietnam, particularly in the mountainous areas in the north of the country.*

Ben O'Connor Croft skiing perfect powder on the lower part of one of the finest off-piste descents in the western Alps, the Pas de Chevre, Chamonix Valley, France.
The west face of the Petit Dru is clearly visible directly above the skier. This iconic peak has been affected by a series of massive rockfalls over recent years, the evidence of which can be seen in the large grey scar on the right side of the face.

High above a lone paraglider over the Glacier des Bossons, Matt Perrier takes no prisoners as he charges the fall-line on Cosmiques Couloir, Mont Blanc, France

January 2010

Chris Savage deciphering the complex blue headwall between the trees on the immaculate *Escalata Master* (8c+/9a), in the Perles Valley, Catalunya, Spain. This extraordinary route lies hidden on an obscure cliff in a quiet valley in northern Catalunya, and is considered to be one of the finest climbs of this standard in Europe by the few people who have climbed it.

October 2010

Murray Dale high above the road on the huge, shady sweep of overhanging limestone at La Croix and the superb tufa climb *Out of Africa* (7c), Gorges d'Aveyron, southwest France.

October 2009

Hazel Findlay suspended from the tantalising tufa fin of *Icarus* (8a), Trebenna, Geyikbayiri, Turkey. In recent years, Geyikbayiri has become one of the most popular places in Europe for midwinter rock climbing, with thousands of superb sport climbs in all grades in a dramatic, mountainous setting a stone's throw from the Mediterranean.

Towers of Silence

The Sandstone Spires of the Broumov Highlands

Stretching along the border of Poland and the Czech Republic, the Broumov Highlands is one of central Europe's enchanted places. Lost in time, these forests are replete with echoes of the illustrated pages of *The Brothers Grimm*. The region is a combination of Alice-in-Wonderland weirdness with a bit of Jack-and-the-Beanstalk grandeur: a magic wood of glimmering sandstone towers that catch the light at different angles through the day. Some seem to defy gravity, where others are hardly visible between great pines, larches, firs and beeches. Most of them, though, stand tall and proud, the silent watchmen of this spookily quiet, half-forgotten, mystical landscape.

Ancient seas hollowed out the sandy sub-soils of Moravia around 200 million years ago to form a series of spire forests, great swathes of current-eroded sandstone monoliths that now lie deep within the arboreal terrain along the northeast border of the Czech Republic.

Climbing started here in the inter-war years: the incredible *1923 Route* on the Lover's Tower at Adršpach [see above] bears witness to the vision of the region's early pioneers. And the extraordinary climbing ethic they developed remains strong today. Its main precepts are: only place bolts where absolutely necessary for belays or protection; don't use any metal hardware to protect the routes as it may damage the soft sandstone; use only *knots* jammed into the cracks for protection where you can't (or just can't be bothered) to place a bolt.

The distinctive character of the climbing in this beautiful hidden corner of Europe is beyond question, as is the climbing culture from which it has emerged and grown.

A number of the region's hardest routes were climbed prior to 1991, before the Czech Republic even existed. The harsh economic conditions under which Czech climbers were forced to operate during the long years of Soviet control strongly influenced the bold, frugal climbing ethic of the region. Many Czech climbers up until the early 1990s were not able to acquire proper rock shoes, let alone the other paraphernalia taken for granted in modern rock climbing. As foreign travel was equally difficult for Czechs under Soviet control, the choice back then was simply climb locally using what was available, or not climb at all. The pioneering development of so many impressive climbs on the sandstone towers of Teplice and Adršpach is therefore doubly impressive for the fact it was carried out for the most part with virtually no proper climbing equipment.

Because of the outrageously bold style of traditional Czech rock climbing, these crags remain quiet and are free of chalk, covered instead by their natural garb of lichen and protected by a thin layer of loose sand, a natural climbing repellent. As such, the sandstone spires of the Broumov Highlands are an adventure climber's paradise, and worth investigating for any climber in search of Europe's routes less travelled.

Top left to right: Jeff Hollenbaugh setting off up the huge chimney on pitch 1 of the *1923 Route* (E1/5.10), Adršpach. | Nic Sellars climbing an E6/5.12+ arête at Teplice. | Nic Sellars demonstrates one of the many 'tower jumps' for which the region is famous. This jump is rated a mere '2' on the local jumping scale of 1–5. There is only one recorded grade 5 jump on Czech sandstone, which remains unrepeated to date.

June 2007

Tom Briggs on the huge arête of *Guillotine* (E6), Adršpach, Czech Republic

June 2007

Nic Sellars climbing an unnamed E2 / 5.10 dihedral at Teplice, Czech Republic. The large bolt below him is the only real protection in the pitch. We found our knot-craft to be somewhat lacking on our trip to the region, and preferred to just run it out rather than trust our jammed knots. That isn't to say, however, that they don't work.

June 2007

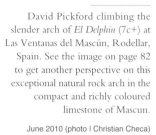

David Pickford climbing the slender arch of *El Delphin* (7c+) at Las Ventanas del Mascún, Rodellar, Spain. See the image on page 82 to get another perspective on this exceptional natural rock arch in the compact and richly coloured limestone of Mascun.

June 2010 (photo | Christian Checa)

Australian climber Helen Day making the crux move of *Coco Loco* (7a+) at sector Surgencia, Mascun, Rodellar, Spain. Over the past decade, the Mascun canyons have become one of the most popular areas for summertime sport climbing in western Europe.

October 2008

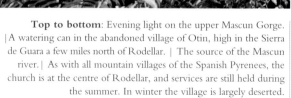

Top to bottom: Evening light on the upper Mascun Gorge. | A watering can in the abandoned village of Otin, high in the Sierra de Guara a few miles north of Rodellar. | The source of the Mascun river. | As with all mountain villages of the Spanish Pyrenees, the church is at the centre of Rodellar, and services are still held during the summer. In winter the village is largely deserted.

October 2008 – June 2010

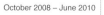

Neil Mawson climbing at Bielsa, Aragon, Spain. Just a few miles from the French border, this secretive cliff is one of the elusive jewels of sport climbing in the Pyrenees, with a host of long, spectacular pitches in a wild alpine setting that rival the best climbs on the more famous cliffs in nearby Catalunya.

October 2009

Semi-fortified churches, like this one at Teurel, at the entrance to the Odessa National Park, are common throughout the Spanish Pyrenees.

October 2009

Neil Mawson climbing the mega-classic *Joe Bar Team* (7c) at Bielsa. This 35 metre route ascends a barrel-shaped wall of immaculate limestone, and is one of the best sport climbs of its grade in Spain – or anywhere in the world.

October 2009

Wind, Sandstone & Stars

Sandstone Solitaire in the American Desert

It was getting late when I turned west off Highway One Ninety-One. Low in the sky, a blood-orange sun began to sink into the vast labyrinths of Canyonlands. Sudden gusts of wind stalked the plains, and the surrounding Mesas darkened as I drove west. The air grew colder as the road dropped off the plateau. Just past the Amerindian petroglyphs of Newspaper Rock, through the corner of the windscreen, I glimpsed a buttress of perfect coloured sandstone fired by the last few minutes of evening light. The rough rock shimmered red, chased by the encroaching shade. Through the gloom, I could just make out the two-tone shadow of a colossal dihedral spearing the cliff. Jet black lines of splitter cracks scored the walls to either side. Instinctively, I pulled over and cut the engine. In the middle distance, the slender towers of the North and South Six Shooter broke the horizon. There was no sound at all except the faint cymbal-roll of the wind in the cottonwood trees. In every direction, high-walled canyons extended into the sandstone tableland, and I slowly came to terms with where I was as night fell across the Colorado Plateau. After years of waiting, I'd finally arrived in Indian Creek, the heart and soul of rock climbing in the American desert.

Nothing you have heard or read about climbing on Windgate sandstone can fully prepare you for the first time you climb on it. American climbers often say that if you think you know how to climb cracks, but haven't been to Indian Creek, then you're in for a big surprise. For your first trip – for the first few days at least – it's a good idea to bear this in mind, and reign in your climbing ambitions accordingly. Before Ray Jardine invented the first active cams in the 1970's, only a few routes had been climbed in the Utah desert by a daring band of pioneers. The reason for this is obvious as soon as you arrive: virtually all the routes follow parallel-sided splitter cracks, which nothing other than cams can effectively protect. The evolution of climbing at Indian Creek therefore mirrors the development of active cam protection.

Getting used to the unique movement of climbing here is a bit like acclimatization for altitude – if you get it right. If you get it wrong, it'll feel more like you've been doing a few rounds with a heavyweight champion wearing a pair of washing-up gloves. At some point, you'll cross a watershed and feel much more comfortable cramming fingers, hands, fists, elbows, feet, shoulders and knees (or a combination of all the above) into the world's most perfect, seemingly laser-cut cracks.

Many seasoned Creek climbers cherish their memory of the day when it all started making sense, and routes which previously had seemed desperate became relatively approachable.

After a few weeks of perfect spring weather in April 2010, the Creek started to feel like home. I climbed many of the classic 5.11 and 12's, and when I finally succeeded on my first 5.13 crack, I finally felt like I was making real progress with the rubix cube of Windgate sandstone.

After a short trip to Zion to climb one of North America's best multipitch routes, *Moonlight Buttress*, I returned to the Creek for a few days. Still flushed with the afterglow of that climb, the place seemed wilder and more peaceful than ever. I climbed a few more classics, but spent more time exploring and photographing the vast maze of Canyonlands and the surrounding desert. The day before I had to leave, a friend and I climbed *North Face Route* on Castleton Tower, the most famous of the freestanding spires in the Castle Valley just north of Moab. From the summit, I kept having to remind myself that I wasn't on an aeroplane: the otherworldly expanse of the Colorado Plateau stretched the horizon's limit in every direction. I stared southwest into the sun, back towards Canyonlands.

It was only then that I began to understand the most painful thing about climbing in Indian Creek – much more acute than the sting of broken skin from the rough sandstone or aching muscles the morning after a long, hard day – is having to leave the place behind.

I drove up Highway Six early the next morning, heading for Salt Lake City and my plane home. As I turned north off the Interstate and across the empty desert of Carbon County, I finally understood that we can only know paradise by knowing what it is like to lose it.

Right: Matty Rawlinson's shadow follows his every move as he sprints up the first section of the hard classic *Sweden Ringle* (5.12) at Indian Creek, Utah, USA
Facing page: A lone rider on a vast wall of purple stone, John Gleason storms up an unnamed 5.10 splitter crack on the far right side of Second Meat Wall, Indian Creek

April 2010

Kate Rutherford turns the arête to gain the
upper crackline of *Family Home Night* (5.12) at
Second Meat Wall, Indian Creek, Utah, USA.

April 2010

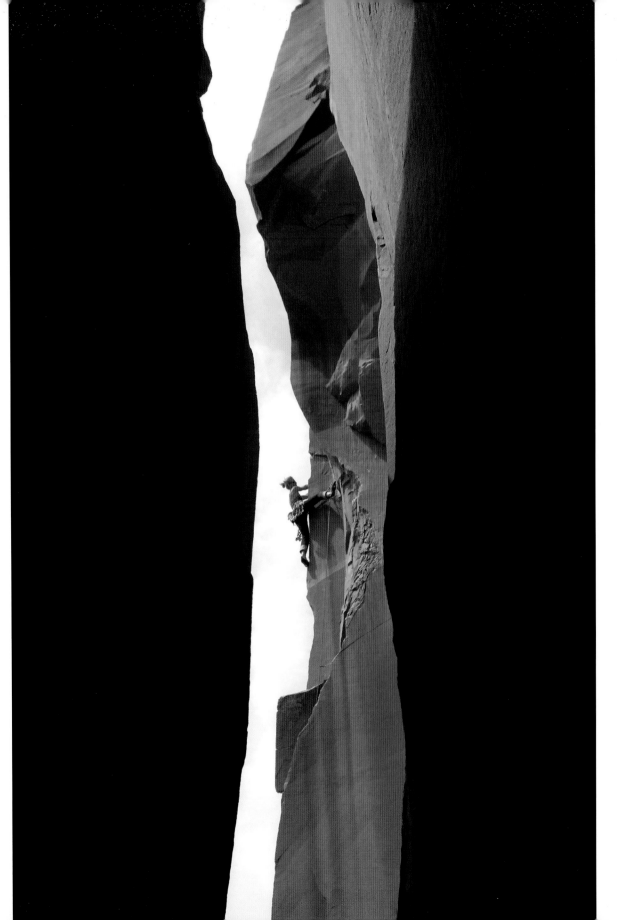

Top left: Kate Rutherford on the lower wall of
Family Home Night (5.12) at Indian Creek, Utah

April 2010

Far left: Petroglyphs at Newspaper Rock, San Juan
County, Utah. One of the largest known collections
of Amerindian rock art in the American southwest,
the first petroglyphs were made around 2,000 years
ago, and left by people from the Archaic, Anasazi,
Fremont, Navajo, Anglo, and Pueblo cultures. These
petroglyphs depict deer, buffalo, and antelope, as
well as likenesses of human figures. Petroglyphs
were carved into rocks, on the walls of caves, and in
sheltered ravines across the Colorado Plateau, and are
a visible reminder of the rich culture and beliefs of the
people who once lived in this part of America.

April 2010

Left: Will Stanhope on the classic off-fingers testpiece
Slice and Dice (5.12), Indian Creek, Utah

April 2010

*Wilderness is not a luxury but a necessity of
the human spirit, and as vital to our lives
as water and good bread. A civilization
which destroys what little remains of the
wild, the spare, the original, is cutting itself
off from its origins and betraying the
principle of civilization itself.*

– Edward Abbey, *Desert Solitaire*

Stone Kingdom of Green

Adventures in Sweden's Granite Neverland

Above: Norwegian climber Hilde Bjørgås hangs the sloping holds on the crux of *Doktor Feg* (Swedish 7+ / E5) at Hella, one of the best crags in Bohuslän
Right: Top Swedish climber Malin Holmberg cuts loose through the huge roof-traverse of *Mad Rock* (8a) at Granitegrotten, Bohuslän

April 2011 [above]

August 2010 [right]

The forest under Skälefjäll was cool and damp the morning we walked up to the wall one last time. Somewhere up there, among the tall trees shrouded in cloud, was one of the most imposing crags of Bohuslän: a north-facing, forty metre escarpment of steep, smooth, shady granite. Big drops of condensed water clung to the silver birch leaves, playing tricks with the shifting light, and steam rose from some of the tallest pines. Our feet skidded from time to time on the bright lichen blanketing the narrow trail. The trees thickened as the wall began to loom in the middle distance, stilling the air and making our breath condense. Puffs of water vapour hovered in space for a second or two before disappearing into the surrounding gloom.

Suddenly, the wall raises its head above the eager pines that claw and lean against its base. And there it is: *Electric Avenue* (9–/8a). The route follows an impossibly elegant parallel seam that rises the full height of the face, culminating in a bulge at the top before morphing into a cavernous water-runnel. It was there just as it had been before, this most perfect of perfect lines; just as it was before I first came here, or before the first climber ever climbed here, or before anyone ever climbed.

The air was still damp and cloying as I tied on, attempting to remember the mysterious sequence I'd found that unlocked its secrets. I started up the first, easy section with a mixture of trepidation and excitement. At the same time as I reached the break where the wall steepens, marking the beginning of the difficult climbing, an unlikely breeze began to shake the canopy of silver birch and pine behind me. It was a strange serendipity, this sudden wind out of nowhere in the middle of a humid August day. Both times I'd tried to lead the line previously, I'd been slapped off the tiny crux holds by the creep of condensation under my fingertips. But this time – my last attempt before I had to leave to catch my plane home – I knew there could be no such excuses.

As soon as I stepped into the awkward fingertip layback that leads into the crux, my fingers felt cool and dry on the holds for the first time. I chalked up once: this time, once was enough. Instead of battling with the holds as I had before, I began to use them with exactly the right amount of pressure. The gear below disappeared into the enveloping mirage of the trees, and at the limit of reach I caught the small edge

at the point where the twin flakes merge into a single, wire-thin seam that cuts through the upper headwall. After another three dynamic moves – feet up, tension, balance, stretch – I'd caught the shallow one-finger pocket just below the horizontal break, the final rest before *Electric Avenue's* last defence.

Here, guarding the door to the top of the crag, an all-out layback off small vertical edges and poor smears allows a good incut to be grasped. I breathed out hard, tightened up, and launched. Before I could register I'd done it, the fingers of my right hand sank into the hold. Both my feet cut loose, skittering across the granite like skimmed stones, and I palmed up into the huge water-worn atrium at the top in astonishment.

Some moments in our climbing lives stand tall above the rest. They're not necessarily the biggest grades, or our greatest or boldest accomplishments. Instead they are the experiences that strongly reflect the choices we've made in order to be there to encounter them: the moments that simply tell you who you are, and why you are here, doing what you're doing today. They are the routes that remind us why we still climb, and why we will always climb. For me, *Electric Avenue* was one of those climbs. It is an incomparably brilliant route, and marked the beginning of a personal journey of discovery that would lead me into the heart of one of Europe's greatest climbing areas, a mystical stone kingdom hidden among the forests and islands of Sweden's west coast.

As I sat at the departure gate in Gothenburg's Landvetter airport a few hours after climbing *Electric Avenue*, I understood that the connection I'd formed with the cliffs of Bohuslän wouldn't fade with distance or time. As the plane took off, the pilot banked to the west, and I pressed my face to the window. Sweden's west coast stretched north beyond the horizon's limit: a maze of narrow channels threaded between the islands, reflecting light against the green blur of the surrounding forest. In a few places, white flashes of granite crags and boulders sparked from the trees and along the shoreline. As we climbed, they merged gradually into the approaching blue of the open sea. After a while, the Swedish coast disappeared completely, and the only question in my mind was of when I'd be back.

As the summer surged on, granite towers hidden between the trees and hills of forgotten islands entered my dreams. Sometimes, shrouded figures beckoned from the dark crystals in the stone, ghostly and strange. The urge to return to Bohuslän grew with every passing day.

A few weeks later, on a cool and blustery afternoon near the end of September, I stood nervously below the huge, impending dihedral of *Rätt Lätt* at Häller. First climbed in 1996 by Swedish trad climbing's visionary modern pioneer, Richard Ekehed, it was Sweden's first traditionally protected grade 9 (or 5.13 / E8). Häller is a cliff that no committed climber can ignore. It has a commanding presence outweighing its moderate size, and its cleanest lines have a monolithic grandeur more akin to an alpine face than to a granite wall barely a rope-length high.

Once I'd battled my way to the top of *Rätt Lätt* the afternoon I arrived back in Bohuslän, I knew I had no choice but to continue the journey of discovery I'd started earlier in the summer. The final crux comes at around thirty metres, at the apex of the steep arête bounding the right wall of the dihedral, and about ten metres out from the last gear at the back of the corner. I forgot my foot sequence on the final, heart-in-fingertip lunge, and very nearly blew the last move, just managing to claw my way to the final fingerjams instead of clocking fifteen metres of airtime.

A haze of mustard fields filtered through the oak canopy, and a glance down at the farm below the crag with its old red Volvo parked outside checked me back gently into reality. As I reached the top, it was clear that Bohuslän granite had become as deeply interwoven into my climbing life as anywhere else in the world.

Later that week, when I reached the top of the classic thin crack of *Catch* (Swedish 7+/E5 6b), on the main wall at Hällinden, the web tightened again. This huge single pitch follows the central crackline that splits a wide expanse of bullet-hard rock, and is as good as any single pitch at that grade I've climbed on Californian granite. Yet, like Bohuslän particularly and Swedish granite generally, this superlative climb remains almost completely unknown outside the small, close-knit Scandinavian climbing community.

As I continued my exploring that autumn, encountering new cliffs and climbs, the diversity of Bohuslän became as clear as its presiding character of magic. We parked by a huge barn full of

Top: British climber Ian Hollows setting up for the crux move of a testing 8− / E5 crackline at Galgeberget, Bohuslän
Lower: Swedish climber Oskar Roshed on the lower crack of *Electric Avenue* (9−/8a+), Skälefjäll, Bohuslän

April 2011 – August 2010

A Finnish climber on the steep offwidth crack of *Off Line* (Swedish 7 / E4) at Häller, Bohuslän

August 2010

rusty machinery on the edge of the woods, walked through a meadow of long grass, and were suddenly in the enormous cave of Granitegrotten. Massive roofs dwarfed the big pines and beeches growing in front of the cliff. Soon I was cutting loose on the wild lip traverse of *Mad Rock* (8a) with abandon, throwing heelhooks and searching for kneebars amid the vast ceiling's outlandish structures. Later that day, with weary arms from horizontal sport climbing, we drove up a dirt road that winds up the hill to the hidden enclave of Välseröd. There, we jammed and laybacked splitter cracks evoking the spirit of climbing in the American desert. Later, we ran down to the sea in the gathering dusk, and perhaps Bohuslän's most beautiful cliff, Ulorna. Rising from a tiny, secret shingle beach on the shore of a long saltwater inlet, the small collection of high standard trad routes here represent all that I had come to love about Swedish granite. The more I explored and discovered of this place, the more my enchantment grew.

Climbing stories should reflect the places we climb in as strongly as they evoke our adventures there: just being in the presence of cliffs and mountains is as important as the routes we climb on them.

Whilst we are all inspired by the thrill of the runout, the focus of the crux, and the finality of the top, every climb is bound up in a complex psychogeography of desire and possession far beyond its mere physical nature. And whilst we all feel the monolithic power of Yosemite's El Capitan when we stand underneath it, or the elemental force of a Himalayan peak as we stare up from a glacier, the immense scale of the most imposing objectives can create a parallel sense of impersonal impregnability. Smaller, less dramatic cliffs often have a stronger effect on our imagination.

There is nowhere I've felt this phenomenon as strongly as among the crags of Bohuslän. As I write this, I can still smell the mossy, mushroomy scent at the base of the cliffs, and see the quicksilver flashes of quartz from the granite as the first sun hits the wall. I can still feel the unmistakable bite of the hard, fine-grained granite as my fingers close on a crimp, and hear the smoky caws of wood pigeons and rooks from the forest as I'm stepping into the first move.

That's the essential magic of the place the Vikings called Ránríki, the sacred land of the goddess of the sea, and Álfheimr, the home of the elf. Climbing has arrived in their realm very recently, yet these presiding spirits of place are old. They've lived among the woods, inlets and islands of Sweden's west coast since the first Viking explorers imagined them there.

Even today, Rán and Álf are still out there somewhere among the trees and stones of Bohuslän. And we should count ourselves lucky that we may still explore the green kingdom of their enchantment.

Malin Holmberg makes a rare repeat ascent of the desperately thin modern trad testpiece *Event Horizon* (Swedish 9– / E8 6c) at Hallinden, Bohuslän

June 2011

Ránríki

The old name for a part of Viken, corresponding to southeast Norway and the northern half of the Swedish province of Bohuslän [the name is also roughly identical with Álfheimr, or 'the home of the elf', in Scandinavian mythology].
The name Ránríki is thought to be derived from the Old Norse goddess of the sea, Rán.

Top & centre: Sea ice on the boulders at Hönö, Västra Götaland, Sweden
Bottom: Lichen shining in the crystal winter morning light at Hönö
February 2011

Malin Holmberg bouldering in warm sunlight and sub-zero air temperatures on a perfect winter's morning at Hönö, Västra Götaland, Sweden
February 2011

Geir Söderin attempting a hands-free ascent of a boulder at Hönö, Västra Götaland, Sweden. Despite the perfect friction of minus five degrees Celcius under a deep blue sky, he didn't quite stick it: there's always one that gets away.

February 2011

Malin Holmberg finding the point of balance on the square-cut and super technical arête of *Razor's Edge* (9–/8a) at Skälefjäll, Bohuslän

April 2011

On a golden Atlantic evening, French climber and alpinist Max Bonniot makes the wild final moves of *Let The River Live* (E6 6b) at Pedn-men-du, Sennen, Cornwall, England, during the 2010 BMC International Meet. The cliff's name translates from the Cornish language as 'Headland of Black Stone'. The far west of Cornwall is a continually changing country, its shifting moods reflected by the Atlantic weather that besets its beaches, cliffs and wild moors. Ocean, stone and sky entwine all who come here.

May 2010

Way Out West
Chance Encounters with Cornish Granite

Returning to west Cornwall, like T. S. Eliot in *Four Quartets*, I find that to arrive back at my starting point on sea cliff granite I begin to know the place for the first time. Bosigran – the proudest of all the crags in the region – is my favourite granite cliff in England, and every time I go back there I discover new dimensions in familiar spaces.

When I was nineteen, soloing a few routes was a logical way to finish a day's climbing when my partner had already expended all their energy. Late one summer evening I ran from the Carn Galver mines to the top of the Great Zawn. As I arrived on the narrow col above the west wall, the heat of the day had given in to lengthening shadows. In a few minutes, I was sliding down the last few metres of rope to land on the boulders heaped at the base of the slab. *Desolation Row* follows the thin cracks splitting its left edge; a clean line rising to the apex of the zawn. It's one of the best E2's in England.

I began climbing almost immediately. Soon, I was high on the slab, balancing carefully on small edges below the crux section, where the crack thins into a spidery seam.

The calm sea glinted darkly from the cavern below, sluicing in the narrow channel at the zawn's entrance. Somewhere overhead, a peregrine shrieked and then swooped out to the west. Bob Dylan's lines began to float in the zawn's ether: 'Between the windows of the sea where lovely mermaids flow… / nobody has to think too much about Desolation Row'. Lifted by that vision, I drifted through the crux and landed back on the col, half-dreaming. Out to sea, an offshore wind blew wide, expanding whorls in the dark water beyond Bosigran Head.

On a roll, I raced back over to the Main Cliff and up Joe Brown's 1957 masterpiece *Bow Wall* (E2 5b). On the crux, swinging from a perfect handjam at the end of the diagonal crack, a peregrine falcon swooped behind me, mobbed by a pair of clamourous ravens. By the time I'd got to the top, he'd shaken them off, and I watched him circling out to sea as a thin vein of cloud crossed the falling sun.

Max Bonniot gets his first taste of British sea cliffs during the 2010 BMC International Meet on the dramatically-positioned *Samson Arête* (E2 5c) at Sennen, Cornwall

May 2010

The disused workings of the Carn Golver mines, high above Bosigran

May 2007

Above: David Pickford making the first ascent of *Teahupo'o* (E8 7a) on the Diamond Face at Bosigran in 2007. Still the hardest route on the cliff, it features a gigantic 'dyno' move to reach the undercut flake seen in the photo, and had not seen a repeat ascent when this book was published in 2013.

Right: Looking southwest towards Cape Cornwall from Bosigran Head on a wild spring day of strong winds and high seas

May 2007

In the spring of 2007, my thoughts returned to Bosigran and to a line that had seen attempts by two of the best climbers southwest England has ever produced, Ken Palmer and Mark Edwards: the extraordinary diagonal seam that bisects the heart of the Diamond Face. Over two days, as high seas driven by an intense low pressure off Iceland thundered into Porthmonia Cove, sending sheets of spray a hundred feet into the air, I unlocked the puzzle of how to gain the seam. Both Mark and Ken had been trying to gain it direct via a desperately hard boulder problem. I immediately discounted this as a viable option, but found a small crimp on the extreme lefthand side of the face, gained from the neighbouring HVS, that allowed an improbable horizontal dyno to be made out right to a very small undercut at the very base of the seam. The crux move itself remains the hardest, wildest, and most unusual I have ever done on any route, including all the sport routes I've climbed. Launching out with a kind of fencer's lunge I could just catch the tiny undercut as I was cartwheeling off the crag, and then clamp the barn-door shut by catching the left arête of the face with my left toe. All that remained after this was the relative sanctuary of E6 laybacking up the seam proper. *Teahupo'o* (E8 7a) is named after the legendary reef break off Tahiti where Laird Hamilton surfed one of the heaviest waves ever ridden in August 2000. It seemed appropriate given the wave-like nature of the line, and the immense ocean swell thundering into the crag that day.

I'll never forget the awestruck feeling of making the first ascent of the hardest route on one of my favourite cliffs in the world. Routes like these – *Desolation Row, Bow Wall, Doorpost, Suicide Wall, Bosigran Ridge, Teahupo'o* – they all explain in different ways the reasons I love rock climbing in general, climbing in Cornwall in particular, and why Bosigran is simply one of the best crags in Britain.

'We spent a blissful new year in Goa, celebrating our survival of the world's most dangerous roads
with an appropriately poisonous-looking bottle of Maharastran rum...'
David Pickford on a V3 highball on the sunrise boulder at Hampi, Karnataka

January 2006 (photo | Jakob Schroedel)

Shakti and Dust

An Indian Journey

'Namaste…? Hello, Mr Singh?'

As I peer through the darkness of Lalli Singh's basement workshop in a sidestreet of Karol Bagh, I break into a gentle sweat induced by the inhalation of stagnant petrol fumes. My hopes of finding our Enfield Bullet 500 serviced and ready to hit the road are diminishing with every breath.

'Hello Mister' one of Mr Singh's affable young mechanics pipes up.

'I am most very sorry good sir, but we have problem. Bike not finished.' The boss, it transpires, is away, and the Bullet won't be ready until the day after tomorrow.

Delhi is the kind of city in which a great deal of time and energy may need to be expended simply in order to get out of it. This is an experience familiar to many climbers heading up into the Himalaya. After a four day epic of multiple high speed rickshaw journeys between Connaught Place and Karol Bagh, the Bullet was finally ready and the prospect of escape from the metropolis, alpine-style, was imminent.

The phrase 'baptism of fire' took on a slightly whiffy irony on the first day of our three month mega-roadtrip around India. Just a few hours outside Delhi, between the bustling plains towns of Ghaziabad and Haridwar, my girlfriend and I found ourselves squatting with an alarming urgency in a large field of sugar cane, attempting to camouflage ourselves from curious locals, as the notorious bacteria of the capital began to take serious effect. After numerous impromptu stops later, our journey gained a nauseating comedy as I steered the fully loaded Bullet at walking pace through a swarm of cyclists and vegetable sellers amid the catatonic traffic of Muzzafaragnar whilst Sarah made impressive arcs of projectile vomit over my shoulder. Amazingly, she took commendable measures to avoid spattering the town's numerous cows with vomit. Cows are sacred to Hindus, and we just escaped the disdain of the local *brahmin* by a combination of her good aim and a few well-timed swerves on my part.

After a few days in Rishikesh recovering from this febrile introduction to motorcycle travel in the subcontinent, and after giving ourselves an even stronger dose of antibiotics, the magnetic pull of the mountain roads of Himachal Pradesh proved too strong for us or the bike to resist.

The air grew steadily colder as we wove through the foothills of the Himalaya, heading westwards toward that troubled frontier country of Kashmir. We emerged from the Jawahar Tunnel into the sharp December sunlight of the Kashmir Valley after surviving over three miles of terrifying icy darkness filled with diesel smoke. Passing various avalanche warning signs, I realised we were in the precarious position of travelling on a motorcycle in the approaching clasp of the Himalayan winter – with only one way out should the first snows arrive.

The weather was fair but the ever-present thought of a cold front coming down from the Karakoram was enough to make our stay in the place Salman Rushdie describes as 'a paradise not so much lost as ruined' a short one. In good weather, the renowned Highway 1 from Jammu to Srinagar is one of India's most dangerous roads. In snow, the bellow of pressure horns erupt from Indian Army trucks as they slide around blind corners above thousand-metre scree slopes (all whilst triple-overtaking bullock carts and clapped-out buses, naturally). Riding a bike on a road like that makes even the most dangerous forms of climbing look safer than tennis.

At around 3 a.m. on the morning of December 12th 2005, the shockwave of an earthquake originating in the Hindu Kush measuring 6.7 on the Richter scale hit Srinagar and generated a series of minor tsunamis on the city's lakes. Woken by this unusual nocturnal intrusion, the seismic wave subsided as our rickety houseboat pitched violently for the last time, and I meditated on the local wives' tale claiming that earthquakes are caused

by the angry writhing of a subterranean serpent. Not being a naturally superstitious person, I am however a keen advocate of respecting local custom, and did not wish to wait and see if the apocryphal snake's powers extended from plate tectonics to the generation of blizzards.

We left Srinagar the following morning – which was later reported as the coldest December morning in Kashmir for five years – wearing every item of clothing we had. Back on the other side of Jawahar Tunnel, and despite almost being forced back through the gargantuan fume-filled pipe by a clamorous posse of Indian soldiers demanding our passport details, visions of imminent frostbite subsided with the first few gusts that came in from the south.

And with that warm air blowing up from the Punjab came hallucinations of a distant country; the granite plains of Karnataka far to the south, and of boulders watching over the ruins of lost empires among the lush green of the paddy fields. With that in mind, the Bullet and its two shivering riders made haste out of the icy claws of the Himalayan winter and south towards the sands of Rajasthan's Thar desert.

A couple of weeks later, having covered 4000 kilometres since leaving Delhi, Sarah and I rode the Bullet into the ivory sand at Mandrem on the Malabar coast on December 30th. The Arabian Sea glinted with preternatural zeal that evening: this must have been what Roman centurions had known, I thought, on seeing the Mediterranean again after long years of battle in distant lands. We spent a blissful new year in Goa, celebrating our survival of the world's most dangerous roads with an appropriately poisonous-looking bottle of Maharastran rum. At last, it was time to escape India's potholed highways and homicidal driving – for a while.

After a break from the road to explore the climbing at Badami and Hampi, we covered a lot more ground. The Bullet took us south from Goa to the Nilgiri Hills of south Karnataka, the Cardamom Hills of Kerala, then west again to the Indian Ocean and Kayakumari in Tamil Nadu, the most southerly point of the subcontinent. From there, we continued south to Sri Lanka.

We headed back north in mid-February as the pre-monsoon heat was already beginning to build, thickening the morning air like swathes of smoke in black bamboo. Sarah had to fly back to England in a week. I had a loose plan to ride back to Delhi over the following month, completing a huge, jagged loop around the country. One afternoon the following week, in the middle of a hot afternoon in the arid heart of India with the monsoon still months away, I turned the Bullet around and headed back to Hampi, first to climb and then to go home. I'd made good time that day from the small village in rural Karnataka I'd left at dawn all the way to the border of Andra Pradesh. By now, I properly understood how hard the road would be up through India's poorest east coast states to Varanasi and on to Sikkim in the eastern Himalaya. As I manoeuvred the Bullet through the chaotic traffic of another anonymous, dirty town somewhere on the high Deccan, I remembered my near miss with that truck in Java three years before and the effects of too much riding, and realised I'd been on the road long enough.

Soon afterwards, I hit the main National Highway that links Bangalore with Hyderabad, where I'd have to fork south and then east again back to Karnataka. Here, I stopped at a little roadside dhobi-stall for chai and a cigarette, and paused for fifteen minutes before riding on.

Left to right: A good road in Kashmir. | An even better road in the western Thar Desert, Rajasthan. | Heading south from Kashmir towards the Punjab, Rajasthan, and Karnataka. | Boulders at Hampi, Karnataka, lit by a midwinter sunset. | David Pickford climbing *Kundalini Rising* (7C/V10) on the Kishkinda Boulders, Hampi, and one of the finest boulder problems in India. | Map reading by a lake in the southern Cardamom Hills, Tamil Nadu

December 2005 – March 2006

In the next hour, just after turning around, I saw the biggest cobra I have ever seen. Curling into the darkness like a scene from the Ramayana, the great snake quickly disappeared into an immense, overgrown well. In India, the hooded cobra, or 'naja naja', is replete with surrounding mythologies; the Hindu god Shiva is often painted with a protective cobra around his neck. Snakes make me superstitious, and just after I saw the cobra I passed by a Hindu funeral procession in a dusty village on the plains. The mourners' songs meandered out into a hot, empty sky. It felt like that huge snake, vanishing as quickly as he came, had come to tell me that I'd reached the end of my journey.

I rode west into a golden blue spring evening as thick clouds of insects descended on the cooling rice fields. After a while, the sun went down over the Deccan and I rode on into the night. As I neared Hampi, frogs croaked through the darkness from the Tungabhadra river as a huge full moon rose over the plains, breaking the drone of cicadas. Above me, towers of pale granite were shadowlit against a night sky pinned with luminous stars. After a while, I stopped by a lone coconut tree and cut the engine. Silence – that most elusive thing of all in the world's busiest country – overcame me. At the end of the very last day of my journey around the subcontinent, I finally understood why India is not just another country, but another way of seeing.

David Pickford bouldering beneath Kyashar, Tangnag moraine, Khumbu, Nepal. I was guiding a commercial expedition on Mera Peak, and as my clients were relaxing and acclimatising at Tangnag I decided to go looking for some bouldering opportunities on the vast moraine beneath the mountain's daunting west face. I found this extraordinary boulder just as I was about to pack my gear and leave. Composed of perfect granite deeply grained with mineral deposits and quartz, and varying in colour from deep orange and rust-red to shimmering silver, it's one of the most appealing small rocks I've ever climbed on.

October 2007 (self portrait)

138

David Pickford bouldering at circa 4300 metres on Tangnag moraine, Khumbu, Nepal. This is a different view (looking east towards the west face of Mera Peak) of the same V6 boulder problem seen in the photograph to the left.
The mist kept blowing in and out as I was bouldering here, creating an ethereal atmosphere. It was just the huge mountains all around, the shifting light, the boulder, and me: a perfect place to practise the art of climbing-as-meditation.

October 2007 (self portrait)

Granito Immacolata

The Secret Glade of Italy

Through the slow heat of an August afternoon, we cross the river and walk through a meadow towards the forest. The air is thick with thunder and the smell of vegetation. Shrouded by tall trees and separated by a series of terraces that ascend the mountainside above, Cadarese is a secluded, secretive cliff – a place that conceals more than it reveals. Pillars of green and silver granite rise between the pines like the bastions of a forgotten fortress. Threads of gossamer and dry leaves float on thermal updrafts, sometimes catching on our chalkbags and in our hair as we climb soaring splitter cracks and shady, serpentine dihedrals. A pine marten leaps from a hanging branch and darts through a narrow cleft between boulders. Somewhere high overhead, a peregrine's shriek breaks the humid silence. Later, we pack up in the gloom as the cliff darkens, but the presence of these gifts hangs in the cooling air as we descend through the woods and wander back to camp in the remaining light.

Hazel Findlay making one of the first repeat trad ascents of the stupendous crackline of *The Doors* (8a+/E8/5.13) on the upper tier at Cadarese, northern Italy, after it was debolted and reclimbed as a trad route by Matteo Della Bordella in 2011. Matteo's impressive, commendable act will hopefully set a precedent for the way in which perfectly protectable crack climbs are approached by European climbers in the future.

August 2012

Top: Maddy Cope twisting between the trees on the lower tier at Cadarese.

Lower: Hazel Findlay turning the changing-corner crux of the beautiful dihedral system of *C'era Una Volta* (7b) on the lower tier at Cadarese.

Right: Maddy Cope launching into the huge, Yosemite-style flake line of *Foglie Cadenti* (6b) on the upper tier at Cadarese, northern Italy

August 2012

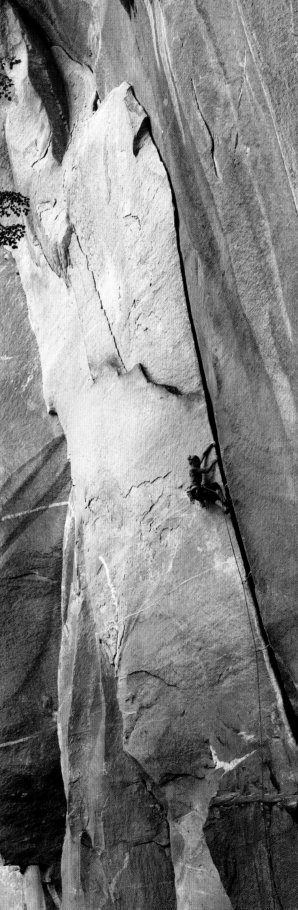

Behind The Lines
Climbing's Invisible Architecture

As the Intercity sped north into the dusky November afternoon, its tail lights faded into an eerie, reddish gleam. The main line out of St Pancras rumbled with the vibrations of other trains approaching and disappearing. Leaning over the parapet of the railway bridge, my six year old feet dangling off the ground, I stared at the space where the railway lines met the horizon. Tracing them slowly back to the bridge, I noticed that their apparent straightness was an illusion: the lines formed a very gentle curve, like the earth's surface seen from space. Just then, the bridge shuddered with the vibrations of another northbound train. I watched as kinks appeared at each of the intersections between its carriages, highlighting the hidden, sweeping arc of the tracks. After a while, the train vanished in the same, strange smudge as the previous one. I jumped down from the parapet, shouldered my satchel, and shuffled off into the gloom of the north London evening. But I must have learnt something on that bridge, because I never looked at a line in the same way again.

In the twenty-five years that have elapsed since then, lines have shaped my life more than anything else: lines of stone, lines of language, and the interplay of lines of light and shadow through the lens of my camera.

The idea of lines is central to the adventurous mindset: defining the course of the voyage on a nautical chart, or the path of a journey through unmapped terrain, lines are the essential tools by which humans find their way and break new ground. Like sailors and explorers of the past, climbers and mountaineers create, follow, and reinvent lines. They may also break, reconnect, and disrupt them. Lines generate our ambitions, distil our fears, and define our successes and failures. We love lines, but we may also fall out of love with them. They can be good or bad, big or small, beautiful or horrible. But whatever or wherever they are, they are the heartbeat of the climbing life, and the cartography of its infinite map of possibility.

When I first looked at the line in Pembrokeshire, Wales, that became *Point Blank* (E8 6c) there didn't seem to be a way through the apparently featureless limestone of Stennis Ford's central headwall. After an hour of dangling on a rope, contemplating moves, the sorcery happened: a single line of weakness appeared in the blankness, a gentle arc swooping through the blue void of the headwall. After making the

first ascent the following day, I stopped for a while on the opposite side of the Ford as my friends walked on.

Looking at the route more closely, I realised the line was just like those railway lines I'd stared at as a boy from the parapet of that London bridge. It appeared almost straight at first glance, but it was actually quite the opposite: kinked and twisted by the forces of nature, its true form only became visible through the movement of a climber across it. *Point Blank* is a line of least resistance through a wall of mirrors, disguising itself like a figure in a masquerade.

All our dances in the vertical are choreographed by the great game of lines. And like the masque, it is a game of illusions, tricks, and shifting identities. This is a sketch of its seven most significant players.

The Perfect Line

The island rides on the Andaman sea like a galleon flagship, its crenellated crest casting a jagged shadow in the dark water beyond the reef. On the east side, a tiny beach fringed with coconut trees skulks under massive overhanging walls of technicolour stone. As our speedboat turns across the sun, I glimpse a single tufa column rising from the beach like an uncoiling snake to the full height of the cliff. If a perfect line is something geology has made into a piece of spectacular rock architecture, then this was it.

The hum of the twin outboards slows to a quiet burble as our boat slows before the reef and the bow sinks into the water. I'm in Thailand in March 2004, and gaze up at the immaculate east wall of Ko Laoliang. Closer to the shore, unclimbed lines rise everywhere I look, linking features like a snakes and ladders board. But the towering tufa system rising directly from the centre of the beach I'd seen from the sea called out more loudly than the rest. A week later, after making various first ascents, I bolted and then climbed the eighty metre line from a hanging stalactite above the sand to the capping jungle at the headwall's limit. The second pitch – which followed a pristine tufa fin for twenty five metres culminating in a bulge like a serpent's head – remains one of the finest sport lines I've climbed anywhere. We named the route *Flying Snake*, after Thailand's Chrysopelea serpents which flatten themselves into aerofoils as they glide silently down from their jungle perches.

David Pickford making the first ascent of *Point Blank* (E8 6c) at Stennis Ford, Pembroke, in May 2008. The climb has since become a sought-after hard classic, and has seen onsight ascents by some of Britain's best climbers including James Pearson, James McHaffie, and Steve McClure.

May 2009

photo | James Marshall

A late rainbow graces the incomparable El Capitan which stands at the heart of Yosemite Valley: the stuff of climbing dreams past, present, and future.

photo | Ian Parnell

The Broken Line

Whilst many of the finest lines are based on a single, continuous feature, sometimes it's the art of locating the missing piece in the vertical jigsaw puzzle that creates a great route: turning a 'broken line' into a major climb is one of the most satisfying experiences in the process of creating new routes. Perhaps the best example of a perfect 'repair' for a broken line is Nico Favresse and Sean Villaneauva's solution to their stunning 2008 Yosemite free route *The Secret Passage*, which finds a way up the hostile righthand section of El Capitan. The name derives from a short section of the 5.13+ (E9) crux pitch which seemed apparently blank until Favresse discovered a tiny seam, just deep enough for his fingertips to hold, which made the entire route possible as a free climb.

In 2004, Mike Robertson and I made the first ascent of *Wall of Spirits*, a bold face climb high on the Great Wall of Pentire in North Cornwall, England. But there was a missing piece in the jigsaw: an independent first pitch that would link into the crux headwall pitch and create a complete route. For two years, the missing piece remained unfixed. I returned in 2006 and climbed an independent first pitch, gaining the ledge directly beneath the crux. With the line complete, *Wall of Spirits* became something more than that isolated pitch on the headwall, and the challenge of the first continuous ascent still remains. Like many of the most appealing broken lines, its history is still incomplete.

The Grand Line

The most powerful example of a grand line is *The Nose* of El Capitan in Yosemite: the most famous route on the most famous piece of rock in the world. Grand lines are routes that keep on giving, regardless of popularity, difficulty, or status. First climbed in 1957 after a massive siege, involving a 15 hour lead through the night by Warren Harding up the final headwall, the free ascent eluded the leading rock stars of the 1990s until Lynn Hill's groundbreaking achievement in 1993. The route's grandeur is shown by its immense popularity today with all kinds of climbers, from big wall newbies to the world's best: the line is iconic, flexible, compelling and accommodating.

Today, *The Nose* remains the focal point in the culture of big wall speed climbing: the current record was set in June 2012 at 2 hours 23 minutes by Alex Honnold and Hans Florine. As arguably one of the finest lines on any rock face in the world, the immense physical grandeur and pole-position of *The Nose* has turned it into the racetrack of choice for big walling's Formula One. The point that the much-coveted 'Nose Speed Record' makes cannot be put down to American exceptionalism alone, or to the inevitable atmosphere of competition in an arena consisting mainly of muscled Bavarians and bronzed Californians.

The line matters, the race seems to say. And it matters a lot.

A line that pierces the desert sky like a thrown knife: Matty Rawlinson on the classic *Gemini* (5.9) Indian Creek, Utah, USA.
The route is a little easier than its namesake in Rodellar, Spain [see photo overleaf], but no less of a landmark for climbers operating at this level.

April 2010

The Landmark Line

Geminis ascends a gorgeous forty metre line of interconnected stalactites, welded calcite patina and fused solution pockets through the steepest section of Gran Boveda, the immense frozen wave of overhanging limestone that dominates the lower part of Rodellar's Mascun Gorge in Aragon, Spain. It's an iconic route, first redpointed by big-wall legend Nico Favresse, and commands centre stage in one of the world's best limestone cliffs. In late October 2009, the first big storm of the coming winter had left some sections of Gran Boveda black with seepage. Malin Holmberg, who's holding my rope on my first proper redpoint attempt, vanishes into a tiny speck on the dusty floor of the cave as I approach the final crux; a powerful, technical cross-through sequence on a sloping, letterbox-shaped pocket. The right edge of the pocket is a slimy mess of chalk paste after yesterday's rain. At the instant my left hand hits it, I cartwheel out into space.

Winter was coming, and I needed to go home, move house, and reconnect with the real world after two months of living as a dirtbag. Early the next morning, I drove out of the canyon under threatening clouds and headed north for France and home. But *Geminis* didn't leave my mind over the hours of solitary driving between the Pyrenees and Calais. The line possessed me through the long months of darkness, and I knew I'd be back to complete it the following year. There was a monumental quality about the line that stood out above other sport routes I'd climbed. As the American climber Alex Honnold once put it to me, 'that downwards diagonal traverse before the crux feels kinda like being on a big wall.'

Eight months later I returned to Mascun with Adrian Baxter, and the two of us redpointed one of the best sport routes I've ever climbed. Landmark lines like *Geminis* are important, because they redefine our perceptions of what we think we can achieve. At the same time, they can change some climbers forever. When Andy Pollitt, one of British climbing's leading talents of the 1980s, moved to Australia in the early 1990s he spent months attempting Wolfgang Gullich's Mount Arapiles masterpiece *Punks in the Gym*, possibly the world's first 8b+. When he succeeded, he promptly quit high level rock climbing forever. For highly performance-oriented climbers, landmark lines can be dangerous: they can create a sense of endgame which leads to a rapid exit route from the sport.

A perfect line: Doug McConnell on the awesome square-cut arête of *Hazard Reduction* (25 / 7a+) at Centennial Glen, Blue Mountains, New South Wales, Australia.

December 2012

David Pickford grappling with tufas on the crux of the king line *Geminis* (8b+) at Gran Boveda, Rodellar, Spain. After thirty-five metres of severely overhanging and very strenuous climbing, the crux of the route involves a cross-through move from the obvious tufa into the sloping pocket just to its left. Like all the best crux moves, it is almost at the top of the climb, failure will result in a huge fall, and it requires composure, focus, and good technique to execute correctly.

June 2010

photo | Christian Checa

Malin Holmberg seconding the amazing flying ramp on pitch 3 of *The Lady of The Lake* (E8/5.13) on Djupfjord Wall, Lofoten Islands, Norway, on the first ascent. The location of the 'invisible fingerlock' I refer to is shown by the green quickdraw on the left edge of the image. Turn to page 178 to read the full story behind this magic line.

July 2011

The Impossible Line

Most unrealised climbs are known as 'projects'. Bizarrely, the term is often used regardless of whether they are actually being attempted by someone. Most of the hardest projects in British climbing throughout the late 20th century were considered impossible by the climbing community until someone, eventually, climbed them. In 1988, Mark Leach named his stunning free version of the aid route through Kilnsey's Main Overhang *Mandela* (8a+), because 'people said it would never go free' like the great South African leader.

The idea of considering lines 'impossible' could be attributed to the special brand of scepticism indigenous to the British climbing community, or to a latent Anglo-Saxon conservative resistance to change. The concept that certain lines will never be climbed has now lost virtually all of its historical currency, largely driven by the explosion of internet climbing media in the last decade and a new awareness of the extraordinary rise in global climbing standards. Even so, hundreds of unclimbed 'projects' scatter the crags and boulders of the world, and some remain perceived as impossible lines.

Probably the most famous impossible line in British climbing is the square-cut, virtually holdless arête at Burbage South in the Peak District known as *Wizard Ridge*. Like many of the greatest hard lines on British rock, it was first envisaged as a climbable route by Johnny Dawes over two decades ago. Given the fact that serious injury or death would be the likely consequence of a fall from the upper part of the route, a lead seems extremely unlikely in the new, 21st century climbing culture where 'death routes' just aren't as cool as they once were.

The Forbidden Line

Mountaineering's answer to the rock climbing concept of the impossible line is the idea of the forbidden line; a route so treacherous that it becomes regarded as completely unjustifiable. The greatest example of such a route is Everest's so-called 'Fantasy Ridge', named by George Mallory due to its otherworldly, unattainable nature. American climber Ed Webster has described the ridge in no uncertain terms. 'It's a very, very long and narrow ridge, *double-corniced nearly the entire way* [Webster's italics], with a really long way still to go to the summit. It's awkward, dangerous, with no options for retreat when things go wrong'. Since Mallory's first acknowledgment of it almost a century ago, it has seen very few attempts – and none of them successful. When the talented team of Dave Watson, George Dijmarescu, and Dawa Nuru Sherpa approached it in 2006 they looked at it for some time before calling the expedition off. When Watson was later asked why they did, he curtly replied 'we came here to climb, not to die.'

Due to the astonishingly rapid progress in the sport over the last thirty years, rock climbers have come to understand that describing an impossible line as 'unclimbable' is unwise. Similarly, mountaineers know that the concept of a forbidden line only really goes as far as the next weather window or the next season. The fundamental objective differences between mountaineering and rock climbing can sometimes separate the two activities, but our attitude to impossible and forbidden lines shows how the two disciplines often merge together at an ideological level. Climbing is a dream-making machine, and it is these unreachable lines that form many of its wildest creations, make its myths, and conjure up its future.

Epilogue: The Magic Line

There's a final kind of line, above and beyond all those that have gone before. They are the ones you haven't yet climbed but which you want to climb, the ones to which you give everything you've got and just succeed, and the ones that you hope to climb, perhaps, some time in the future. I've been lucky enough to have climbed a few magic lines in my climbing life, perhaps because I've spent a lot of time thinking about them and searching them out.

There is peculiar wizardry about free lines on big cliffs which link features together by the narrowest of margins. Sometimes, they are so remarkable that they lead even a committed atheist like me to believe divine forces might be at work in the geological universe. Near the top of the third pitch of a new route I climbed in Norway's Lofoten Islands with Malin Holmberg, *The Lady Of The Lake* (a 250 metre E8/5.13) I was presented with an impasse before a tiny ledge three metres above me. If I could reach it, I knew the route would link up as a free climb. But if I couldn't, it wouldn't. As is often the case on granite walls, there would be no other way to link up the features. I spanned out from undercuts, and my fingertips sunk into an invisible fingerlock, allowing me to reach the ledge in a couple of moves. It was a sure sign of the line's magical characteristics which culminated in a one-in-a-million crux pitch high on the headwall.

In the same way that the true nature of those railway lines I'd watched as a kid was only revealed by close observation, magic lines often have something of the invisible about them, a magnificent hidden architecture that only becomes evident at close acquaintance.

The climbing life allows us to enter a world of immeasurable richness and beauty, and magic lines distil the essence of what we seek when we climb. Shaped by nature and crafted by our endeavours, these mystical routes are the true art forms of the vertical world, and the catalysts of climbing ambitions that span continents, styles, and generations. Of all the myriad structures in the vertical world, magic lines are its strangest forms. They represent all we dream of, all we accomplish, and everything else we have to lose.

Courtney Sanders approaching the powerful crux moves of the ferociously fingery *God's Own Stone* (5.14a / 8b+) Red River Gorge, Utah, USA

Tales From The River
Climbs on Kentucky's Wild Side

'So they ain't gaat naa ice where y'all come from, boy?'

I look up from photographing the 1950s soda machine outside Kooks Grocers and Gas to see the old redneck leering down at me with bulging, bovine eyes. His drawl is thickened by his complete absence of teeth, his hands shoved deep in the pockets of filthy dungarees. The unmistakable shape of an automatic pistol hangs heavily from his right hip.

I don't think he's here to talk about the weather, but he seems harmless enough. I gesture vaguely at the machine, and tell him where I come from most things like that were thrown in the trash a long time ago. He shrugs, shakes his head, and shuffles off towards his truck with one hand on his gun, as if to reassure himself that it was still there.

Powell County, Kentucky, is one of the poorest places in North America. Adult illiteracy runs at around 18%. Ramshackle trailers with boarded windows sporting 'No Trespassing' signs line minor roads. The guys wear guns on their jeans, spurs on their boots, and the girls wear their hair like it's 1984. Baptist churches cast weird shadows across the dirt of deserted parking lots where kids hang out, watching the road, waiting for something to happen.

Powell County is also home to the greatest sport climbing area in the United States: Red River Gorge. The quantum shift between the rural poverty of the Bible Belt and world class sandstone just a stone's throw away is one of the great contrasts in North American climbing. If you make the effort to travel here, you'll probably have an experience you won't forget for years – even before you touch rock.

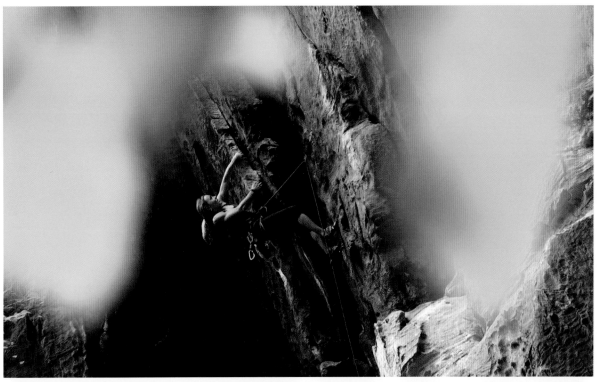

Top: Between the trees at Drive By Crag, a Spanish climber makes light work of the initial layback of *Head and Shoulders* (5.11d / 6c+)

Lower left: The sign outside the Powell County 'Beer Trailer'. Powell is a dry country and liquor cannot be sold at bars or restaurants.

Lower right: You have been warned… most locals in Powell County prefer to uphold the Second Amendment to the United States Constitution, the right to keep and bear arms. It's therefore probably not a very good idea to trespass on their property.

Right: The classic line of *The Force* (5.13a / 7c+) at The Dark Side showing the unique texture and complexity of the Red's sandstone architecture.

October 2012

Swedish climber Malin Holmberg soloing the beautiful hidden line of *Quien Sabe?* (VS 4c) at Bamford Edge, Peak District, England, as the last light of a winter's day leaves Ladybower Reservoir in the valley below. It was here that the Royal Air Force tested Barnes Wallis's dam-busting 'Bouncing Bomb' in the early 1940s using Avro Lancaster heavy bomber aircraft as part of Operation Chastise, which destroyed the Möhne and Edersee dams in Germany's Ruhr Valley in 1943.

November 2010

Gritstone expert Adam Long making the precarious final stretch for the top of *Art Noveau* (E6 6c or highball V6), a famous micro-route on the upper tier of the Roaches, Staffordshire.
The six-metre line, first climbed by gritstone visionary Johnny Dawes, is typical of the small but perfectly-formed nature of many gritstone climbs. First climbed with a rope and led with small wire protection,
it is now usually climbed 'highball' style with multiple crash pads and spotters. With the bouldering boom – and the new approach that has come with it – many short routes have been transformed into very exciting boulder problems.

October 2010

Tim Emmett climbing into the falling sun on *Chouca* (8a+) at sector Bout de Monde, Buoux, France. The first ascent of this iconic route was made by Antoine Le Menestrel, a professional dancer, in 1984. The climb has since become one of the most celebrated and sought-after sport climbs in the world, and defines the revolution in rock climbing standards that took place in the 1980s.

February 2011

Polish climber Aga Banazec cranking it out under a thundery summer sky on the superbly-positioned blunt prow of *L'Escamarla* (8a) at Siurana, Catalunya, Spain

June 2010

Paul Riley on the massive blunt arête of *Episode* (7b) at Manjo-Carn's sector classique, high above the Aveyron river and the Gorges d'Aveyron, southwest France. The prominent cliff visible on the opposite side of the river is Le Capucin, the Aveyron's most famous crag.

April 2009

Sarah Garnett concentrating on the precarious crux of the technical face climb *Souvenir de Bleau* (6c), Gorge du Tarn, southwest France, high above the green water of the Tarn river and the roof of the medieval chapel immediately below the crag.

August 2008

Andy Long emerging from the darkness of the steepest section of *Infinite Gravity* and into the light of the upper arête. After 20 metres of upside-down climbing, there is only another 20 metres of 45-degree overhanging climbing to go. This huge line is the most overhanging single pitch of climbing in Britain, and one of the finest creations of long-standing Dorset activist Pete Oxley. Pete made the first ascent of the route in 1990 using homemade bolts, and I made the second ascent in 2000 (using the decayed bolts and other gear to back them up). The climb has since been retro-bolted, and has seen ascents from some of Britain's more adventurous sport climbers. The situation and character of this stupendous climb is completely unique, and an ascent will be remembered forever.

August 2011

Matt Pickles reaching the end of the initial groove of *Infinite Gravity* (8a+) at Blackers Hole. Only a mere thirty metres of spaced-out, upside-down climbing await him above here…

Far left: Dave MacLeod making the third ascent of Tim Emmett's super route *Muy Caliente!* (E9/10 6c) at Stennis Ford, Pembroke. The name means 'very spicy' in Spanish, and you'll know what spicy means when you're running it out for the gear before the crux. Although the route has now seen a number of ascents (including an incredibly bold ground-up ascent by James Pearson, the most impressive ground-up climb ever made in Britain) the greatest challenge still remains: to place a habanero chilli pepper in the mono-pocket before the crux and to consume it, whole, as you climb past it. The first climber to complete this feat will be worthy of the respect of the legendary fire-breathing Welsh dragon itself.

September 2011

Left: Simon Tappin placing a microwire to protect the crux of *Oratario* (E3 5c) at Misty Walls, Pembrokeshire. Located just a few minutes' walk from Huntsman's Leap, the easy approach and open aspect of this cliffs means it is the perfect respite when rapture of the deep in Huntsman's Leap (see pages 158–163) reaches fever pitch.

June 2008

Bonita Norris running it out to the top of *Marion* (HS) on a windswept spring day on The Promontory at Baggy Point, Devon, England

May 2011

David Pickford on his route *The Nightfishing* (HXS/E7 6b) on the Cheesegrater Wall at Baggy Point, one of four hard, unconventional trad routes he established on this extraordinary thirty metre wall of colourful, gently overhanging shale. The other three climbs are *The Dark Dialogues* (HXS/E7 6b), *The White Threshold* (HXS/E7 6c), and *Headcleaner* (HXS/E6 6b). Most shale is very loose, but the Cheesegrater cliff is an exception: eroded by constant interaction with the sea, the rock is fairly compact underneath its friable surface, and offers difficult, sustained and strenuous climbing with some reliable protection. None of these four climbs had seen a repeat in 2013.

April 2005 (photo | Mike Robertson)

Nic Sellars making a precarious rockover move beneath a lonely peg runner on the bold, magnificent slab of *Inferno* (E5 6a) on The Long Rock at Baggy Point. Lundy Island (see pages 98–101) can be seen on the horizon in the distance.

May 2011

Ian Parnell soloing the soaring crack system of *Shangri-La* (HS) on The Long Rock at Baggy Point

December 2007

Above: David Pickford on the crux section of James Pearson's intriguingly-named route *Do You Know Where Your Children Are?* (E8 6c) on the west face of Huntsman's Leap, Pembroke, Wales. The line is a harder, direct version of *Dusk Till Dawn* (E7 6b), which gains the pink headwall from the open groove to the left (the line of Pat Littlejohn's testing E7 *Terminal Twilight*, probably the hardest trad route in the world ever climbed without chalk). **Right:** David Pickford making the cross-through move out right to gain the pink headwall on the first ascent of *Dusk Till Dawn* (E7 6b) on the first ascent in September 2010.

Above: August 2011 (photo | Neil Mawson) **Right:** September 2010 (photo | David Reeves)

Rapture of the Deep

The Visionary Darkness of Huntsman's Leap

Conception

The horse stamps his hooves and snorts as the rider pulls him to a halt. Surveying the clifftop, the huntsman traces its contours for signs and clues. The low winter sun flashes off the steel barrel on his rifle as he steadies the horse. Out to sea, squalls scud across the sky and darken the waves. Lundy Island – an enclave of brigands, bandits, and Barbary pirates – appears and vanishes through the mist. A pair of choughs quarter the open ground between the horse and the cliff's edge.

As they pass, the rider notices a long, low depression in the ground about two hundred yards ahead. Like the shadow of a submerged whale, it reclines in diametric perpendicular to the cliffline among the thickets of gorse and heather. To landward, the shadow widens to suggest the presence of a chasm below, presenting what appears to the huntsman as the opportunity for an epic show-jump.

A wild-eyed young daredevil, he can't resist the temptation to attempt the giant leap. Acknowledging the rider's proposition, the horse senses his boldness and makes a single, powerful snort.

At the exact moment of that signal, he digs his heels hard into the animal's flanks, and the pair of them surge forward into the sun.

Clods of ripped earth fly into the air and land with muffled thuds. Down in the deepest reaches of the chasm, the thunder of the horse's hooves begins to echo, increasing dramatically until it overwhelms the din of the sea.

Then an immense black shape fills the air. High above the sea, weightless for a moment, and with the horse's charge bearing him forward headlong, the huntsman is filled with an exalted freedom.

White riders on the pale sky. White horses beyond.

Initiation

It was late one summer Sunday afternoon by the time Mike Robertson and I were racking up on the flat grass above Huntsman's Leap. I was seventeen, and felt as if I'd just landed on another planet.

Down in the depths of the chasm, climbers were making their way up some of the classic routes: *Shape Up, Bloody Sunday, Beast From The Undergrowth*. Chalked holds made unlikely connections in the gloom and wove patterns across the coloured stone, white against red, merging into complex hieroglyphs at certain cruxes. The spooky names of the harder routes echoed like ghostly voices in my head: *Minotaur, Headhunter, Snake Charmer, The Witching Hour, Souls, Boat To Naxos, The Black Lagoon, Terminal Twilight, Hunter-Killer, Woeful.*

As you descend into the Leap there is a distinct drop in temperature as the sun only touches its sandy, boulder-strewn floor for a few hours each day. Once immersed in its depths, you enter a transitory, tidal space of exquisite beauty and mystery.

I set off up *Minotaur* (E5), a statuesque climb that pierces the brooding heart of the west wall, weaving through its welded conglomerate channels and weird parabolic bulges like monstrous ice cream scoops. As I gazed above, sinuous cracks threaded through frozen serpentine structures of red and orange stone. Reflected light from the pools of seawater left by the falling tide glinted off the wall, washing the boulders with oily liquid.

Twenty minutes later I topped out, blinking in the white light as I emerged from the shadows. As the afternoon turned to evening, I leaned on the whale-shaped block under the west wall, belaying Mike as he made his way up *Headhunter* (E5). The tide had started to come in, making small surges between the boulders which rolled together and boomed like steel drums. In the cooling air, I shivered in my thin shirt: we were the only climbers left in the Leap. Right then, a big Atlantic grey seal with a scar on its nose swam in on the tide. He stared straight at me, and then up at Mike with intense curiosity. Above him, a host of awesome climbs waited in prescient silence, like sleeping giants frozen in ice. Little did I know that this introspective chasm would shape my climbing ambitions for years to come.

Neil Mawson peering up to find a way into the gloom of the crux chimney on *Darkness at Noon* (E5), Huntsman's Leap, Pembroke, Wales.
This classic extreme of Pembrokeshire, established by British sea-cliff pioneer Pat Littlejohn, takes a wild trip through the deepest reaches of one of Britain's most unusual coastal features.

August 2011

Rapture

You don't have to engage in battle on a climb to know catharsis; it can come from a more joyful source. In many of our most memorable moments on the cliffs, we experience something like rapture. And the more I climbed in Huntsman's Leap, the more that rapture grew. By the summer after my first visit, I started to venture on the harder routes. High on the bold arête of *Compulsion* (E6 6a), far from the RP's I'd placed twenty feet above the boulders, I stared into the smooth looking-glass of the wall. Onsight climbing is often about following threads, hoping they will be long or strong enough to eventually tie together. As I traced the microscopic seam leading up to my left, I tried to imagine possible holds and gear. Because human beings are neither wizards nor angels, our conjuring tricks seldom work out the way we'd like them to. Standing on poor smears at the limit of my reach, the fingertips of my left hand hit a positive edge. I closed them into a crimp, too far out and committed to reverse the move now, and stabbed my feet up. Juddering into balance in a tiny scoop, barely in control, my blood surged with release.

Two years later, on a balmy Sunday morning in mid-April, I'm definitely not feeling like climbing a big, bold route in the Leap after an all-night party at Trevor Massiah's house in nearby Stackpole. Unfortunately for me, my partner that day and the most enthusiastic person in British climbing, Tim Emmett, had other ideas.

Spurred on by his enormous psyche, soon I was cleaning the barnacles off my shoes and chalking up below the ultra-intimidating line of *Nothing To Fear* (E7 6b), Martin Crocker's brooding testpiece on the left side of the west wall. As it had before, and as it would so many times again, the Leap cast its spell. I suddenly found myself at the crux; a weird, strung-out sequence on bad sidepulls and insecure footholds. With more gas in the tank than I'd dared to imagine, and Tim's voice encouraging from the darkness beneath, I floated into the deep runnel marking the end of the hard climbing, and screamed with surprise as I rugby-tackled the cornice of overhanging ivy at the top.

An hour later, my hangover returns as I find myself holding Tim's rope on George Smith's characteristically butch and bizarre line *Woeful* (E6 6b) which lies under the boulder choke in the depths of the Leap. Having long cut off any hope of escape, the tide is lapping at my feet as Tim fights the beast in the black space above. After a while, he vanishes completely into the darkness. A series of long, guttural groans echo from the depths. By now, the sea is washing around my knees. Thoughts of drowning loom as I'm almost submerged by the biggest wave yet, and yank myself up instinctively on the belay for a precious gulp of air.

Soon, Tim's belayed on the boulder-choke that separates the Leap's landward and seaward sections. Climbing fast to shake off the shivers, I pass the crux with a series of seal-like slaps, and reach the signature move of the routes in the deepest reaches of the Leap: a 'controlled fall' from one side to the other, the object of which is to form a body-bridge with your feet on one side of the chasm, and your hands on the other. Spreadeagled in this way, the climber can bypass terrain that would otherwise be impassable. The rock in the Leap's innermost depths has a strong green pigment, and colours the water in dizzying jade and emerald light. Moving through this secret region as the reflected light off the sea illuminates the visible darkness all around is one of the great experiences in British climbing.

Perhaps this was why the pioneers of deep sea diving called nitrogen narcosis 'rapture of the deep'?

Matty Rawlinson on the bold and technical headwall of *Fitzcarraldo* (E5 6a) on the east face of Huntsman's Leap, Pembroke
May 2010

The crux move of *Dusk Till Dawn* (E7 6b) on the west wall of Huntsman's Leap, Pembrokeshire. I made the first ascent of this line in August 2010. A harder direct start to the route was added by James Pearson in 2011, *Do You Know Where Your Children Are?* (E8 6c).

August 2010

photo | Alastair Lee

Recitation

Every time I've climbed with soloist extraordinaire Jules Lines, outlandish ideas have turned into convoluted adventures. One spring day in 2006, driven on by Jules's undiminished appetite for breaking new ground, I found myself racking up below *Minotaur*, with the vague idea of gaining the unclimbed hanging runnel in the headwall above its crux. I had already sneaked a look over the lip of the headwall on a rope to remove the giant cornice of ivy that obstructed the summit. From there, I'd spied an improbable sequence of moves leading out left from the welded jug after *Minotaur's* crux. It looked like it might go, or it might not: such is the way of many of the most appealing unclimbed routes.

Reaching the crux of *Minotaur*, I realised just how steep the moves leading into the runnel actually were; rock always looks steeper when you're underneath it. I wove what was left of my rack into a web of placements around the jug, chalked up, and swung out left. Catching a sloper at full stretch, I flicked my left toe up to a high smear. Barndooring quickly, the point of stable balance long past, I lunged for a solitary crimp and caught it as both feet popped, only just holding the deadpoint. The upper runnel floated by in a dream-haze, and *Theseus* (E6 6c) held sway in the final battle.

Resolution

As the years flew on, my fascination with the Leap grew into a sometime-summer obsession. I found new territories in the sequestered patterns of its stone, new kingdoms in the cool air of its darkest reaches. Fast-forward to 2010, and I teamed up with Dan McManus for an attempt at the gorgeous-looking unclimbed headwall to the right of Pat Littlejohn's masterpiece *Terminal Twilight* (E7 6c) which may well be the hardest trad route in the world first climbed without chalk. After the first ascent, Pat capitulated to the white powder and established another hard Leap classic, naming it *The White Hotel* (E6 6c).

Swinging around on the abseil rope, I discovered a pair of strange twin pockets to the right of the final niche on *Terminal Twilight* that allowed access to the headwall. The crafty passage through the water-sculpted flutings and the giant cyclops-eye pocket that create the link to the top offered some of the best climbing I've done in Pembrokeshire. After a battle with damp rock on the sustained lower section, I managed to hold it together and topped out in golden evening light. Realising that the new line, *Dusk Till Dawn* (E7 6b), was probably the best thing I'd climbed in the Leap at that point, an intense calm overwhelmed me as I belayed Dan in the gathering gloom on *The Pulsebeat* (E6 6b). As he neared the top, darkness was falling, and a big Atlantic grey seal swam in towards the beach on the rising tide, just like the one who came on my very first evening in the Leap. Rolling in the water with effortless ease, the seal's sudden presence articulated what I already knew about this place, and everything else I didn't know. Great mysteries remain undeciphered on these shadowlit walls. Some could produce climbs so futuristic that when completed they will become testpieces for future generations, as the Leap's hardest lines are today for ours.

And along with the realisation of such routes, new climbers will come here in search of Britain's greatest limestone trad climbing. I have visited this cathedral of the sea for the last fifteen years, and will continue to return for as long as I can. Perhaps that's the measure of a truly great cliff – somewhere you can find peace and potential at any stage of your climbing life. Or perhaps it's more the measure of the Leap's distinctive kind of magic, that rapture of the deep you always find down there in the darkness of a summer's afternoon.

The crux move of *Minotaur* (E5 6a) on the west wall of Huntsman's Leap, Pembrokeshire. In 2006, I made the first ascent of a direct finish to the route with Julian Lines, *Theseus* (E6 6c), which moves left at the chalked-up holds just above the climber and into the steep runnel beyond.
August 2011

Top: Huntsman's Leap, Pembrokeshire, on a falling spring tide.
Centre: A karabiner and part of a mortar round from the nearby Castlemartin Firing Range salvaged from Huntsman's Leap show the corrosive effects of salt water.
Lower: Rapture of the deep: Pat Nolan rejoicing at the end of a fine summer's day in Huntsman's Leap.

On the same day Barack Obama was elected President of the United States, an Argentinian climber powers out of the roof of *Darwin Dixit* (8b+) lit by the golden glow of the late autumn sun at sector Laboratory, Margalef, Catalunya, Spain

November 2008

A lonely climber silhouetted against a radiant midwinter dusk as he moves up the imposing stalactite columns of *Colonist* (8a+), one of the classic climbs of Geyikbayiri, Turkey. The mountain catching the last light in the background is Geyik Sevrisi (1750 metres).

January 2011

Sarah Garnett a hundred metres above the turquoise water of the Mediterranean on the crux third pitch of *Sole Incantore* (6c+) on the Aiguilla at Cala Goritze, Sardinia, Italy

May 2005

Swiss climber Katja Barrueto finds an ingenious solution to the serpentine 'changing-tufas' crux of *Rattlesnake Saloon* (7b) at Trebenna West, Geyikbayiri, Turkey

January 2011

166

Tim Emmett poised above the swirling waters of the Green River on the immaculate arête of *Catchin' The Wave Train* (5.11c / 7a) at the recently-developed cliff of Suicide Bluffs, British Columbia, Canada. Situated between Whistler and Pemberton, the crag requires an unconventional approach: a tyrolean traverse on an in-situ cable across the rapids to reach the secluded escarpment on the other side.

July 2012

A perfect introduction to rock climbing: the immaculate, arrow-straight splitter of *Klahanie Crack* (5.7 / VS) at Shannon Falls Wall, Squamish, British Columbia, Canada

June 2012

Malin Holmberg turning the lip of the huge roof of *Medidas Desesperadas* (8a+) in the caves of St. Lorenc de Montgai, Catalunya, Spain

December 2010

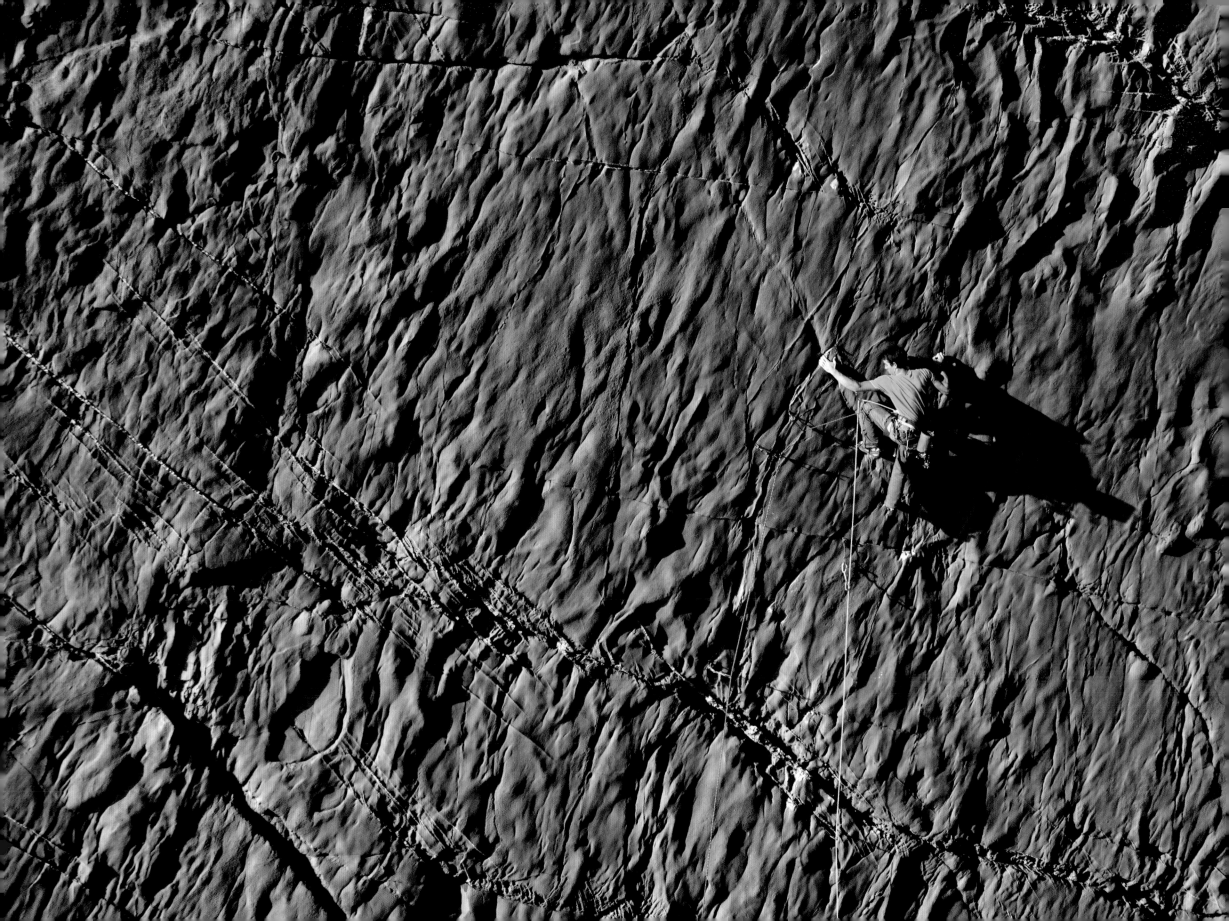

Alex Honnold, the world's most accomplished free soloist, making a quick onsight ascent of the scary southwest classic *Coronary Country* (E6) at Lower Sharpnose Point, Cornwall, on a flying visit to England in spring 2012

April 2012

Hazel Findlay climbing the lower section of *Coronary Country* (E6 6b) at Lower Sharpnose Point as the light leaves the awesome south face of Middle Fin.

April 2012

The surreal fins of Lower Sharpnose Point fired by the last light of a spring evening.

April 2012

David Pickford making the second ascent of *The Monk's Satanic Verses* (E8 6c) at Lower Sharpnose Point in 2000. The climb remains the hardest on the crag, and despite several repeats has not yet seen an onsight ascent.

August 2000

photo | Mark Glaister

Tim Emmett reaches the upper crux of *Chouca* (8a+) at Bout de Monde, Buoux, France, as evening shadows race up the wall below. The climb is one of the finest – and hardest – of its grade in France, and is a stern test of power and technique.

February 2011

An Argentinian climber high on the awesomely-positioned and very challenging climb *Cous Cous* (8c), one of the signature lines of El Makinodromo, El Chorro, Andalucia, Spain

January 2012

Gavin Symonds makes the crux moves around the lip of the ten-metre roof on the obscure but brilliant British sea cliff testpiece *Solid State Logic* (8a) at The Promenade, Swanage, Dorset, England

April 2012

Hazel Findlay making the third ascent of *Once Upon A Time In The South West* (E9) at Dyer's Lookout, Devon, England. This awesomely smooth fifty metre slab rises on the sombre north side of the Lookout's jagged promontory, and is one of the hardest routes on Devon's Culm Coast. It was first climbed by Lake District legend Dave Birkett in 2010, and was the hardest trad climb led by a woman in Britain at the time of publication in 2013.

June 2011

Malin Holmberg seconding the remarkable 'flying ramp' on pitch 3 of *The Lady of the Lake* (Norwegian 9– / E8 6c, 220m) on Djupfjord Wall, Lofoten Islands, Norway, during the first ascent. The first five pitches of the route were climbed onsight, ground-up. The final crux pitch was practised by Holmberg for two days prior to her successful headpoint-style ascent. No bolts or pitons were used for protection or belays, and the route still awaits a repeat and a continuous ascent.

July 2011

Fjord Fandango

Exploring in Norway's Lofoten Islands

The North

I wake to the Sunday morning light at a quarter to five. Last night's traffic is silenced and gone. The midsummer air smells of the streets and the harbour and of the dirty wild flowers that grow along the edges of the tramlines. I open my eyes. Birdsong drifts through the window of our tiny flat in downtown Gothenburg, Sweden. In a blaze of red hair, Malin's already up, and the scent of fresh coffee drifts through the room. Here, I rise to a different life.

The solstice just past, we're drawn north to Norway's Lofoten Islands. Uddevalla. Trollhätten. Fredrickstad. Oslo. The names on the signboards make hidden signals as we pass beneath them, gold and blue, reminding me of the interplay of sun and shadow on Bohuslän granite. Before I made my first journeys to Sweden last year, I hadn't understood the real power of light and darkness. In Scandinavia, they define the course of the turning year, forming a natural reflection of the vast duality of human experience: summer and winter, home and exile, love and death.

One of Europe's longest roads, the E45 runs for almost a thousand miles north from the fertile land of Sweden's southwest coast to the barren tundra of Arctic Norway. By evening, we're leaving behind Storuman, its windows bolted and shuttered as if the town itself were already preparing for the long, isolated months of winter, shutting out the surrounding forest's featureless gloom, the drone of its mosquitoes, the rank stench of its endless bogs, and the impossible vastness of the world beyond.

Midnight. The sun rolls along the horizon when we reach the edge of northern Scandinavia, where the forest gives way to tundra. Huddles of reindeer have long replaced passing cars. Small groups break as we pass; the animals try to shake off mosquitoes with our slipstream.

3 a.m. I open my eyes just as Malin drives over the crest of the hills south of Kiruna, and the morning sun hits the central extraction tower of the world's largest iron mine. The Arctic summer light sparks off the quartz shards of humped slagheaps that loom above the town like a monstrous UFO. A mirror of mine debris covers the mountain, and as we turn across the sun, the reflection fills the windshield, blinding us for a moment, then melting across the dashboard into pools of quicksilver and spilt mercury. It is a moment of such extreme, sudden beauty we both remain quiet. We turn again and descend toward the town, passing sidings of rusting trucks and the snowmobile salvage yard locked in the bright, sleepless silence of the early morning. Winter grips Kiruna for most of the year. Summer is a stranger here, a traveller from the south country, like me. Only a native can understand the true nature of the isolation of this place at the top of the European continent, or what it's like to spend a winter in one of its hyper-insulated, narrow-windowed, Soviet-style apartment blocks. Malin grew up here. Her dad worked in the mine for forty years, hacking iron from the guts of the surrounding mountains. As we turn into the driveway of her family home, she says with a slow, curious smile, 'I know this place.'

After a few hours' sleep, we drive west beside the railway that freights out thousands of tons of iron ore every week. The tundra shines in the morning sun. Stendhal once wrote that beauty is the promise of happiness. The first glimpse of Norway's northwest coast seems like a physical expression of this idea. To the west, south and north, a concatenation of mountains and islands stretches into the far distance. Sharp outlines cut the sky and sketch patterns in the blue ocean. We find a stopping place to sleep late in the evening by the shore. Beyond the boulder-studded dunes, the wild grass blows in the salt wind, and the sound of the sea picks up between the gusts. Gulls fill the air with wheeling cries. Hearing their calls under the midnight sun, we feel free.

For the first few days, we climb classic routes. A white-tailed eagle soars behind us on the final pitches of an elegant thousand-foot line of interconnected corners and arêtes. The sun swings around the corner of the wall as we prepare to descend a shady dihedral, washing the slabs with amber liquid hundreds of metres below. Tiny wooden houses perch on the edge of the harbour balanced on delicate stilts. Out to sea flocks of gulls make high arcs over bright red fishing boats, scattering as they descend. Crennelated lines of mountains stripe the space between the horizon and the sky in a hundred layers. Everywhere we look, and everywhere we are, light and life surround us.

Malin Holmberg leading the crux final pitch of *The Lady of the Lake* (Norwegian 9– / E8 6c, 220m) on Djupfjord Wall, Lofoten Island, Norway, during the first ascent. This extraordinary feature, visible with the naked eye from the fjord far below, is a very shallow, thin seam in an otherwise blank face high on the cliff's imposing headwall, just deep enough for fingertips, and taking only microwire and TC3 cam protection.

July 2011

The Fjord

As we drive around the coast road to Henningsvaer, a north-facing wall shadows the calm waters of Djupfjord. A thin seam splits the centre of its upper headwall. 'Look at that!' I exclaim to Malin as I pull over.

'Imagine if we could climb it directly, finishing up there.'

I point up at the seam.

'I wonder if it's climbable? It looks amazing!' she replies. Her eyes sparkle with silent, spirited energy as she looks up towards the headwall. As she looks back at me, a bright, curious smile spreads across her face.

We run along the shore of the fjord with binoculars to try to get the best view. Tracing the line of weakness from the base, I link features through the strange perspective of 300% magnification: a deep chimney, a bottomless flake, a flying ramp, a crack-corrugated wall, then a rising traverse to the base of that quixotic seam. Even through the binoculars, I can't tell how thin or deep it is. It could be straightforward, or impossible, or anything in between.

After a rest day, we pick a route through the boulders along the shore, up around a rocky bluff, through dewy moss and cloudberries, to find the fixed rope that leads down the other side. Djupford Wall rises above us in all its shady glory. I contort up the dripping, water-worn chimney, finding a belay in a niche after fifty metres. Then Malin sets off up the booming flake that forms the second pitch. As she laybacks the huge tooth of granite, the sun hits the water of the fjord below. I follow her lead with cold feet, wondering what lies ahead.

On the third pitch, I shuffle up the ramp that rises into the heart of the wall like a stairway suspended in space. While I fiddle with mircowires and small cams, I try to forget about my frozen feet skidding on the fresh, thick lichen. Metres out from my cluster of tiny placements, just at the point when I don't want to run it out any more, I spy a widening in the seam and a better cam placement a few metres above. I sprint for it and breathe deeply as my fingers sink into the first perfect jam on the entire pitch. The ramp narrows to the left and vanishes into an ocean of blank stone. My only hope is a ledge five metres higher. Searching for clues, I glimpse a shallow depression to the right, and I span out from undercuts to another perfect finger jam: a gift of nature. Without it, there was no way I could have reached the ledge free.

At the belay, we try to warm our feet. Creased with tiny cracks, the wall now sweeps toward an atrium where the angle will ease and the final seam will appear. Malin's fingers slip in precarious fingertip jams, and her shoes skitter on small crystals, but soon she's moving up toward the golden light that floods across the upper cliff. I check the time: 5 p.m. The wall will now be in the sun until just before midnight, when it dips for just two hours below the ridge to the north of the fjord before rising again.

As I climb toward her, warmer now at last, clouds blow in and blot out the sun. Huddled in her tiny belay niche, she's shivering with cold. I give her my balaclava and wind jacket.

We can see the headwall seam, now, seventy metres above us. From here, it looks perfect. Drainage water runs down the lower cracks from the summit slopes. I meander up a twisting path toward the headwall as the mist thickens below. After a while, I pause to take my bearings: the only way to gain the seam is a wild traverse across the apex of the capping slab. Again, I search for clues, and again the wall gives just enough: a rail of tiny, rippled edges leads me rightward, and I arrive on the sloping ledge beneath the incredible seam.

The cloud has come down around us, and the wind picks up to a near-gale. With chattering teeth, Malin places a micro-cam in the seam as the first drops of rain fall. I suggest we take the easier finish up the wide crack to the right and return for the final pitch the next day. She flashes a smile between her shivers and agrees.

By the time we've reached the base of the wall, the weather has cleared, and the wind-rippled fjord has settled to a translucent calm, reflecting the serrated shadow of Budalstinden high to the east. I show Malin the time: 1:30 a.m. Her sharp green eyes soften with tiredness. We look back up at the line we've just climbed and smile. It's all there in front of us: all 220 perfect metres. The midnight sun is hidden below the bulk of Vestvågøya that blocks the horizon to the north. Silence fills the fjord in the brief Arctic summer twilight, only broken by the crunch of small stones under our feet and the call of a lone night bird that echoes among the rocks and across the surface of the water.

Two days later, the morning air is so clear that simply drawing breath feels like taking an overdose of magic. A short storm blew out by midnight, leaving bright lines of surface runoff cascading from the highest slabs. The sun is already drying off the upper section of Djupfjord Wall. I know I'll never be able to free the tiny seam with my big fingers. Malin, though, has a good chance with her thin hands and crack-climbing mastery. We rappel in to the base of the seam. Malin cleans her shoes. We both take a deep breath, and clasp our hands into fists before touching them together, our habit before a hard lead.

'Okay, you're on. Go for it.' I say. 'Full attack.'

'Yeah. I'm going.' she replies. And she goes. Fighting from the very first move, she hesitates before pulling hard on a flared fingertip jam into a layback. Her foot skids on some lichen, and her hand slips slightly, and for a moment, I think she's going to fall. Instead, she holds the slip and steps up strongly. Two transitional laybacks allow her to swap sides, facing left then right, making the best use of the seam's slight curvature. Many more desperate moves lead to a respite at a slight depression. Resting on the first real foothold since the belay, she places the first gear for many metres, and we both relax for the first time since yesterday. She pauses for a few minutes, breathing hard, then launches out again. On the final hard section, her feet dance across the slab while she makes long, fast reaches between poor fingerlocks. After a while, a scream of joy breaks through the sound of the wind ruffling the hood of my smock. She's made it.

Looking down the final pitch of *The Lady of The Lake* as the midnight sun touches the summit slabs and the fjord far below is cloaked in darkness. Somewhere down there, Malin is busy practising the desperate climbing up the shallow seam on the final pitch of the climb prior to her successful ascent.

July 2011

Djupfjord Wall rises directly from the dark water of the fjord. *The Lady of The Lake* takes a line up the centre of the steepest central section of the face.

July 2011

The Gift

An hour later, we're at the base of the wall again, and I'm cleaning lichen and moss from a steep finger crack that blanks out by a pair of old aid bolts in the very toe of Djupfjord Wall. As I begin to climb the crack, a sudden wind picks up off the fjord, displacing the humid, leafy air, and I know I'm in luck. Long spans lead between shallow, positive locks to a resting place where the aid line goes right. I move up and left on undercuts, and the crux sequence stares sternly down at me. I span out and stab my left forefinger into a razor-sharp mono that winks from the blank wall like a sneering Cyclops. Then I run my feet high on the grainy granite and launch out. I just catch the first of a rail of slopers in a flared horizontal break with the fingertips of my right hand. Feet skittering across the holdless wall, I make a series of wild slaps until I can throw my left heel up, place a cam, and, finally, relax.

The upper crack is easier, although I must clean it as I go. My hands slip from flared jams in the lichenous crack. Soil and decomposing crud pour down my T-shirt. I grope over the top and land on a flat terrace. I can hardly believe it: in one afternoon, we've climbed two of the best granite pitches I've seen anywhere in the world.

Long swatches of evening mist swirl over the fjord while Malin leads a slim pillar split by a thin crack. The sun's just dipped below the opposite ridge. A melancholy chill washes over me as I realize the dusk will come earlier every day from now until the sun disappears completely from the north Norwegian sky sometime in late November. But we've had one of the best climbing days of our lives, so I should be grateful for it all.

Midnight. The sun rolls unseen beneath the cloud-capped mountains to the north. There's a hint of magic about this summer evening under the indigo sky, and for a moment, Malin and I are held still in the breathless rush of the turning world. After a quick, warm, forgetful kiss at the last belay, we're descending through the vertical beech forest that fringes Djupfjord Buttress. Deadwood snaps around me and fresh branches recoil everywhere, as if the forest were closing up behind us as we move. When we contour the steep slope near the toe of the wall, Malin lets out a cry of joy, and I run over to find her kneeling on a ledge covered in bright orange cloudberries: a final gift from the fjord in the fading light.

As we devour them, the sugar rush from the sweet berries makes us giddy, and we roll around on the springy grass like a couple of kids. Malin's eyes are bright with laughter and fire. I know that soon we'll be driving south into the night, leaving all this behind, going back to wherever it was we called home. But home in the climbing life is elsewhere. It's not a place you stay, but a place you find. And you must leave it sometime and pass it on to someone else, so that they too might discover joy and freedom there. Robert Lowell thought

The end and the beginning. The sky at 2 a.m. on the fjord at Kalle, Lofoten Islands. I took this photograph in the final days of our three week expedition in Lofoten, and for me it captures the magical realm of the north Norwegian coastal mountains. As Edith Wharton said, 'there are two ways of spreading light: to be the candle or the mirror that reflects it.'

July 2011

that happiness was something with a girl in summer; I'd take that cloudberry ledge and a beautiful girl anytime over some high-minded ideal of a better life.

The next morning, we drink coffee in Henningsvaer and listen to the news on the radio. Anders Behring Breivik has shot dead sixty-nine Norwegian teenagers in a terror attack on Utøya Island; the most deadly massacre by a single individual in Western Europe since the Second World War. The spell of the magic islands breaks. Against this mindless destruction, neither home nor happiness matter much. In search of silence, we drive north to Eggum where we'd slept three weeks before. Lost in the space between memory and forgetting, we climb a few short pitches beneath leaden skies. Invisible under banks of mist, huge breakers surge on the grey shore. I can't stop thinking about all those kids, their young lives so brutally snatched away. Then I think of my friend Woody, killed in a freak accident on a Welsh sea cliff four months before. And of my grandmother, back in England, now close to the end. Waves of absence crash over me, bearing the open water between the living and the dead. We pack up and leave the cliff in silence. As we drive south, it starts to rain.

We arrive back at Djupfjord in deepening twilight. The weather's cleared, and we walk along the beach that separates the fjord and the open sea. Malin stops to find bright stones among the seaweed and driftwood. A few men and women are fishing on the seaward side of the breakwater, casting out with long rods in the hope of catching a skulking cod or a bass as it silently enters the fjord on the midnight tide.

I walk to the end of the beach and dive into the cold sea. That sudden rush of saltwater across my body washes away the presence of the dead. I swim as far as I dare into the bay before my head burns and my movement starts to slow. Djupfjord Wall looms on the skyline to the east, shrouded now in darkness and mystery. I think of all the harder climbs it still contains, and of how lucky we were to be the first to climb into the heart of this sublime, mysterious cliff.

The light is fading fast as I turn for shore. Lenticular clouds gather on the surrounding summits like flying saucers, casting violet shadows on the dark water of the fjord. Malin's standing on the beach, alone and beautiful, looking out to sea. As I swim toward her, I'm reminded of that far greater gift than climbing – simply being here at all.

Summary: The Lady of the Lake *(E8 / 5.13, 220m) and* Trapezium Wall *(E7 / 5.13-, 90m), Lofoten Islands, Norway, Malin Holmberg and David Pickford, July 2011, first ascents. No bolts or pitons were placed for protection or belays on either route. The Lady of the Lake still awaits a second ascent and a continuous ascent. During the same trip, Holmberg and Pickford also made another first ascent on the central section of Djupfjord Wall,* Norwegian Wood *(E4 5.11, 220m) follows a line of cracks roughly twenty metres to the right of* The Lady of The Lake.

Self-portrait at close of day, Geyikbayiri, Turkey

January 2009

James McHaffie abseils off the impending wall of *Mission Impossible* (E9 6c) on the remote, seldom-visited cliff of Craig y Rhaeadr, Ogwen Valley, Snowdonia, Wales, after making the second ascent of this demanding Neil Carson route from the late 1990s. Perhaps Britain's best all-round rock climber of the early twenty-first century, James has repeated almost all of the hardest climbs in Britain.

May 2009

Under a brilliant winter sun, John Alcock balances up to one of the myriad satellite summits of Hound Tor, Dartmoor, England

February 2008

Malin Holmberg, Hilde Bjørgås and Josephine Rosenberg cast long shadows across finely-textured granite at the end of a glittering spring day at Häller, Bohuslän, Sweden

April 2011

Maddy Cope defying gravity on a sunset run above Cheddar Gorge, Mendip Hills, Somerset, England

June 2012

181

Survivors

Silence remains, inescapably, a form of speech

– Susan Sontag

Ghost wharf in midnight sun, Härnäset, Bohuslän, Sweden

June 2011

Parasol and Buick Roadmaster (circa 1950), El Capitolio, Havana, Cuba

March 2007

Emerging tyre in quicksand, Bridgewater Bay, Somerset, England

November 2006

Left and above: Wreckage of the Vennerne, Rhossili beach, Gower Peninsula, south Wales.
The photographs show the remains of part of the hull (above) and stern (left) of this 275 tonne Danish barque, wrecked on Rhossili beach on 24th October 1894. The captain and all of the crew survived.

May 2013

Copper cans still in use at a rest stop,
Powell County, Kentucky, USA

October 2012

Raeburn in a disused shed,
North Cadbury, Somerset, England

June 2013

186

Exterior of an open bakery in the old town
of Fribourg, Sarine, Switzerland

July 2012

Detail of a working hundred year-old mechanical saw
in an alpine barn, Giétroz, Valais, western Switzerland

August 2012

Late night skater, central Barcelona, Spain

October 2011

Broken signpost at a snowbound junction, Mendip Hills, Somerset, England

February 2009

Road sign used for target practice, near Zion, southwest Utah, USA

April 2010

Working diesel pump at an independent garage,
Kettlewell, North Yorkshire, England

August 2009

Fisherman at close of day, Nigeen Lake, Srinagar, Kashmir, India

December 2005

Marwari nomad and camel bound for Pakistan, western Thar desert, Rajasthan, India

December 2005

Snow squall over Llanthony Priory,
Brecon Beacons, Wales

January 2007

Surviving mangroves six months after Hurricane Helene, the most powerful
Caribbean hurricane of the 2006 hurricane season, Cayo Juntias, northwest Cuba

March 2007

Tobacco field and barn, near Pinar del Rio, west Cuba

March 2007

Light on an empty chapel, Capel-y-ffin, Llanthony Valley, Black Mountains, Wales

January 2007

Fiat Panda outside a house,
San Rocco, northern Italy

August 2012

Mini at rest in a field, Horta, Azores, Atlantic Ocean

Summer 2009

photo | Gavin Symonds

Austin Sheerline (circa 1950),
Clifton, Bristol, England

April 2013

Detail of a working gasoline pump,
Smoky Mountains, Utah, USA

April 2010

Bench in a garden near the sea, Isle of Purbeck, Dorset, England

May 2013

Three chairs outside a petrol station, Finale Ligure, Italy

November 2011

Vespa at the beach, San Vito Lo Capo, Sicily

April 2013

Gate before a snow squall, Mendip Hills, Somerset, England

February 2009

Split tree in clearing fog, North Yorkshire, England

December 2006

Light in an empty door, Sankar Gompa, Ladakh, India

August 2009

Fisherman in yellow and blue, Emporios, Kalymnos, Greece

May 2011

Dye trader at a morning market, Pashupatinath, Kathmandu, Nepal

October 2007

Starlings in flight, Ortigia, Sicily
November 2007

Ghost bridge near Camarasa, Catalunya, Spain

November 2010

Nineteenth century graffiti, Teplice,
Broumov Highlands, Czech Republic

June 2007

Carved faces of unknown origin on a hidden ledge, Gorge du Tarn, Cévennes, southwest France

August 2008

Detail of a working fishing boat,
Bideford, Devon, England

September 2007

Swimming place in midnight sun, Bohuslän, Sweden

June 2011

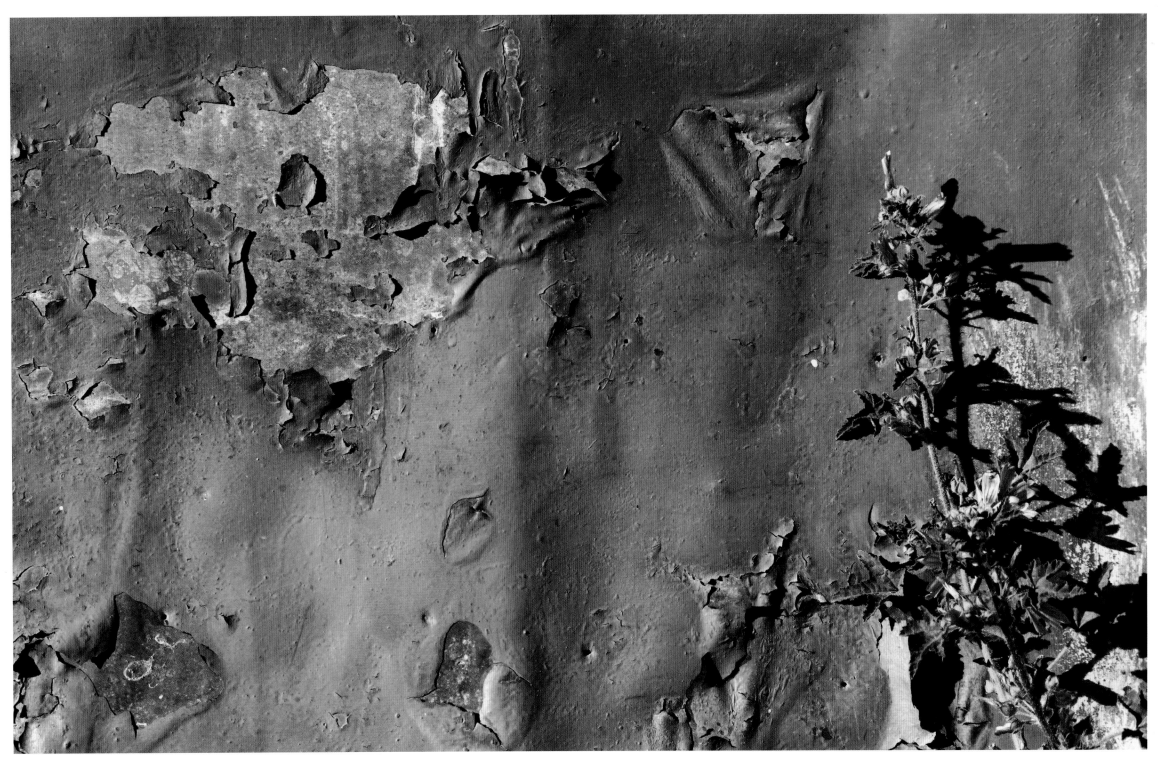

Purple and green on painted corrugate, Abella de la Conca, Catalunya, Spain
November 2010

The Plaza del Toros (Bull Ring) at close of day, Ronda, Andalucia, Spain

January 2012

Last light on the ruins of the old hospital, Lundy Island, Bristol Channel, England

September 2007

Donkey grazing on a salt flat,
Nubra Valley, Ladakh, India

August 2009

Dancing prayer flags, Kote, Nepal

October 2007

Solitary chorten, Nubra Valley, Ladakh, India

August 2009

A monk carrying firewood at circa 5200 metres above Khare, Khumbu, Nepal. The prominent snowcapped mountain in the distance is Malanphulan (6573 metres).

October 2007

Whale vertebrae on a beach, Jökulsárlón lagoon, southeast Iceland

July 2007

Fisherman heading home in an incoming storm, Konyaalti, southern Turkey

January 2011

Wild swimmer in midnight sun, Bohuslän, Sweden

July 2010

Moorish watchtower at nightfall, near San Vito Lo Capo, Sicily

April 2013

Alpine church on a summer evening, near St Anton, west Tyrol, Austria

July 2010

Standing stone of unknown origin, Tsaranoro Massif, Madagascar

April 2008

Working dinghy at low tide, Bohuslän, Sweden

April 2011

Morning light on a working slipway,
Golfo di Cofano, Sicily

April 2013

Ruins of an abandoned house above Golfo di Cofano, Sicily

April 2013

213

Jetty used by local fishermen, Palionisios, Kalymnos, Greece

May 2012

Autumn light falling on an abandoned village, northern Sierra de Guara, Spanish Pyrenees. There are hundreds of abandoned villages in the high Pyrenees, the majority of which were continuously inhabited for hundreds of years until very recently. Some were abandoned as late as the 1980s.

October 2009

Hurricane survivor, Cayo Juntias, west Cuba

March 2007

Heartwood after landfall, Jökulsárlón, southeast Iceland

July 2007

Antlered oak in autumn twilight, Westonbirt, Gloucestershire, England

November 2010

Hydraulic Engine House (constructed 1888) on a spring evening,
Underfall Yard, Bristol, England

April 2013

Alcove after the call to prayer, Jama Masjid, Old Delhi, India

August 2009

Church door in a narrow alley,
central Palermo, Sicily

November 2007

Nineteenth century houses, Grotte di Mangiapanne, northwest Sicily

April 2013

Bicycle as a white submarine, central Copenhagen, Denmark | Operational windlass, Bohuslän, Sweden

January 2013 | June 2011

Kaiser Wilhelm Memorial Church, Breitscheidplatz, Berlin, Germany. The original church was built in 1895, and suffered serious bomb damage in 1943 during WWII. The original height of the church was 113 metres, but its remains (to the right) were much foreshortened after the bombing. A new tower (to the left) designed by Egon Eiermann was added in 1961. The two separate buildings, one from the late nineteenth century and the other from the mid twentieth century, can appear at certain angles to be a single structure.

February 2010

At the centre of our moral life and our moral imagination are the great models of resistance:
the great stories of those who have said no

– Susan Sontag

Detail of a cabin in Freetown Christiana, Copenhagen, Denmark

January 2013

Acknowledgements

Ian Parnell, Ed Douglas, Malin Holmberg, Tim Emmett, Hazel Findlay, Alex Honnold, Jack Geldard, Giles Cornah, Charlie Woodburn, Kate Rutherford, James McHaffie, Simon Tappin, Sam Whittaker, Geir Söderin, Chris Savage, Chris Doyle, Murray Dale, Paul Riley, Dave MacLeod, Neil Gresham, Jeff Hollenbaugh, Bonita Norris, Andy Long, Nic Sellars, Bob Hickish, Matt Pickles, Christian Checa, Gavin Symonds, Adrian Baxter, Tom Briggs, Sarah Garnett, Matt Perrier, Ben O'Connor Croft, Neil Dickson, Neil Mawson, Will Stanhope, Paul Twomey, Steve Monks, Mark Glaister, Doug McConnell, Mike Robertson, Trevor Massiah, John Gleason, Matt Rawlinson, Ramon Marin, Chris Savage, Vince Day, Helen Day, Adam Long, Max Bonniot, Katja Barrueto, Hilde Bjørgås, Josephine Rosenberg, Kate Rutherford, Ian Hollows, Courtney Sanders, John Alcock, David Moore, Tanya Moore, Simon Lowe, Ray Wood, Kate Burke, Alex Messenger, Shane Ohly, Simon Cardy, Tom Rowland, Bernard Newman, Jakob Schroedel, James Harrison, John Coefield, Camilla Peevers, Madeleine Cope, Jonathan Griffith, Sandra Ewert, Christian Beckwith, Steve Berry, Matt Parkes, Andy Whittaker, Amanda Symonds, Gill Wootton, Charlotte Davies, Jim Perrin, Stephen Goodwin, Hugo Glover, Jon Barton, James Harrison, John Quantick, Nathan Ryder, John Pickford, Mary Jane Wallis, Katie Ives, Stewart Wallis, Aga Banazec, Grant Wright, and the others whose names I do not know:

– thank you all for making this book possible –

ARTEMIS MEDIA

Design by
smudge